Organizational Policy
Development

Organizational Policy Development

Guidelines for Establishing Purposes and Procedures

M. Scott Norton

ROWMAN & LITTLEFIELD
Lanham • Boulder • New York • London

Published by Rowman & Littlefield
An imprint of The Rowman & Littlefield Publishing Group, Inc.
4501 Forbes Boulevard, Suite 200, Lanham, Maryland 20706
www.rowman.com

86-90 Paul Street, London EC2A 4NE, United Kingdom

British Library Cataloguing in Publication Information Available

Library of Congress Cataloging-in-Publication Data

Names: Norton, M. Scott, author.
Title: Organizational policy development : guidelines for establishing purposes and
   procedures / M. Scott Norton.
Description: Lanham : Rowman & Littlefield Publishing Group, [2023] | Includes
   bibliographical references. | Summary: "This book focuses on the paramount
   importance of policies and regulations for successful governance operations in any
   organization"— Provided by publisher.
Identifiers: LCCN 2022045445 (print) | LCCN 2022045446 (ebook) | ISBN
   9781475864649 (cloth) | ISBN 9781475864656 (paperback) | ISBN
   9781475864663 (epub)
Subjects: LCSH: Strategic planning. | Management.
Classification: LCC HD30.28 .N6777 2023 (print) | LCC HD30.28 (ebook) | DDC
   658.4/012—dc23/eng/20221103
LC record available at https://lccn.loc.gov/2022045445
LC ebook record available at https://lccn.loc.gov/2022045446

Contents

Preface

WHY THIS BOOK WAS WRITTEN

Factors such as the present COVID-19 pandemic have served to disconnect normal communication practices in all organizations, including educational. What purposes are to be accomplished and what administrative regulations are of vital importance for giving some direction to ongoing program activities? School districts nationally are not well organized. Some parents want their children in school settings, while others seek a safer climate in the home. Best practices for dealing with present climate conditions are not readily available. Learning at home has been implemented in many school districts, while thought is given to what really is the best thing to do. School boards are in the best position to determine best practices. Such practices need to be set forth in the school district's policy manual.

Purposeful policies are of paramount importance, and helpful administrative regulations loom important for giving some stability for serving students at this time in history. Effective policy and regulation considerations can lend some direction for dealing with current and future changes that affect learning climates for students. The important purposes of program activities must be set forth in the organization's official policies. The successful achievement of these purposes is determined by the specific regulations that accompany the policies.

HOW THE BOOK IS ORGANIZED

The book is organized into four chapters. Chapter 1, "Organizational Failure and a Primary Cause," focuses on the paramount importance of policies and regulations for successful governance operations in any organization. The basic problems facing policy development in educational and other organizations are discussed in depth. Important terms related to policy development and implementation are emphasized, and the topics of local control are italicized.

Chapter 2, "The Constructs of an Effective Policy Manual," centers on the specific content commonly required in effective policy statements. Policy compliance is demonstrated by policy examples, with special attention given to local school boards. A policy exercise is included in the chapter to gain the active input of the reader. How an active policy development process can heighten the control of the organization's governing body is detailed.

Chapter 3, "Policy Implementation in Organizations," discusses the importance of having highly competent governing board leaders, the language of school policies, and how school board policies must support the primary purposes of education, that of student learning. Organizational culture and climate are discussed in detail. Both characteristics have major impact on successful policy development and implementation and, ultimately, on the key factor of student learning.

Chapter 4, "Examples of Policy Manuals," sets forth specific examples of quality policy manuals in a variety of organizations, including businesses, industries, and nonprofit organizations. Policy manuals established by universities are included, as well as policies that include regulations within the main policy set forth. An excellent example of a university policy manual is also included.

Chapter 1

Organizational Failure and a Primary Cause

THE SINE QUA NON OF EFFECTIVE GOVERNANCE

The primary goal of this chapter is to underscore the vital importance of a policy and regulation manual for establishing the primary purposes and procedures of successful organizations and to clarify the important terms that are all too often misused in daily practice.

The term *policy* is commonly misused by persons in management positions. For example, a school principal might be heard speaking of a school's policy when, in fact, he or she is referring to an administrative regulation or perhaps a local school rule. The result becomes a confusing factor in the communication with the school's faculty, staff, and students.

What might be your definition of the term *policy*, and how might it relate to or differ from such common terms as practices, orders, principles, procedures, requirements, regulations, laws, or standards? Or are these terms, when used in education, synonymous?

This chapter considers these terms and others that are commonly misused in practice. What is a policy or an administrative regulation? Is the term *policy* synonymous with the term *procedure*? Assume that an elementary school principal, for example, sent a memo to the staff stating that the school is adopting a new policy for retaining a student in grade. Is the statement correct and legal? Policies and regulations do differ and are among the terms clarified in detail in this chapter.

The Basic Problem Regarding Policy Development

School districts in the nation have solved their policy problems. Or have they? In the large majority of cases, a school board simply purchases policy manuals completed by their state school boards association. The state school board's version of school policies is distributed to each teacher, who places their copy on a shelf in the back of their classroom, where it lies collecting dust. Of course, local school boards can add, subtract, or change the policies set forth in the state school board's version, but this action is seldom taken seriously. As a result, almost every school district in the state has the very same school policies.

Why do so many local school districts purchase their policy and regulation manuals? One primary reason is the lack of know-how on the part of the elected members of the school board, as well as frequent school board member turnover, lack of staff time, lack of know-how on the part of administrative leadership, lost factors relating to consulting services, pressures by teacher involvement viewed as being troublesome, and school board attitudes that view policies as being too restrictive.

Nevertheless, the question of whether or not school districts and businesses should purchase what has been termed *boilerplate policies* always comes to the table when the topic of policy development is considered. COMPROMISE (2013) expressed the opinion that although purchased policies can be useful in suggesting content that should be included in such documents, they tend to focus on policy development, and the importance of administrative regulations is needed.

Not all school districts within any one state are exactly the same. Faculty and community involvement in determining a school district's policies are minimal at best. As a result, commitment to the application of the policies by the local schools in the district is an important missing factor. Written policies have always been the sine qua non of a soundly organized and efficiently operated school board. The need for an effective system for keeping policies up to date has been accentuated by the many changes and developments brought about in education since the early 1960s, and again during the many months of the recent pandemic.

A detailed discussion of policy development in K–12 school settings is set forth in chapter 3.

The Specific Characteristics of a Policy

A *policy* is a statement that an organization establishes to set forth its primary purposes. An organizational policy centers on the question of what it is that the organization wants to accomplish. It is a statement that sets forth the goals and objectives of an organization so that its members can use them to operate their roles effectively. In this sense, a policy is an organization's statement that serves to guide its members as they carry out their related responsibilities. Effective local school district policy development is essential for retaining control of the school community's stated purposes.

Organizational policies are highly beneficial to an organization for many important reasons. Perhaps the leading rationale for having school policies is vested in their importance for clarifying why the organization exists. Questions such as: *Why do we exist? Whom do we serve? What are our primary purposes? How best can we serve our stakeholders?* can be underscored by policies that give direction to the organization's ongoing program decisions.

The Specific Characteristics of an Administrative Regulation

A *policy* answers the question of what to do, while an *administrative regulation* answers the question of how to implement the policy. Thus, regulations are directly related to policies in that they set forth the process of using a policy in practice. Policies are established by the organization's governing board, while administrative regulations commonly are recommended by the administrative personnel in the organization. Nevertheless, the common practice is for the school board or a company's board of directors to examine and approve the administrative regulations that have been developed primarily by the administrative personnel.

It must be made clear that the actions of the administrative personnel are delegated to them by the organization's governing board. From a legal standpoint, only the school board, or an organization's board of directors, has the legal authority to "govern" administrative regulation development. The governing board commonly delegates regulation development and implementation to the organization's administrative personnel. It must be made clear that regulations on occasion are placed within a stated policy, and this action is done when the board has a specific procedure in mind that it wants carried out in relation to the policy in question.

A Learning Quiz for Additional Clarification

In the quiz below, label each of the statements as to whether it has the characteristics of a policy or of an administrative regulation. That is, does the statement express *what* purpose is to be achieved, or does it serve to answer the question of *how* to implement/accomplish a purpose? This quiz is set forth as a learning exercise. The statements do not necessarily reflect effective school district policies or regulations. If you do not know the correct answer, do not just guess. The correct answers are set forth and explained at the end of this learning exercise.

1. Don't shoot until you see the whites of their eyes. Policy____ Regulation____
2. Don't shoot until you have a sure shot. Policy____Regulation____
3. It is better to give than to receive. Policy____Regulation____
4. Don't step on the grass. Policy____Regulation____
5. Honesty is the best policy. Policy ____Regulation____
6. Put your money where your mouth is. Policy____Regulation____
7. Do your job to the best of your ability. Policy___Regulation_____
8. Our work should show improved results on each assessment. Policy____ Regulation____
9. Deliveries are to be made to each customer on Wednesday of each week. Policy____Regulation____
10. If you don't succeed, try, try again. Policy ____Regulation____
11. Homework assignments for each student will be assessed and evaluated. Policy____Regulation____
12. All instructional personnel shall be regularly available to assist individual pupils for a substantial amount of time both before and after scheduled class hours. Policy____Regulation____
13. All classroom teachers should be in their classrooms 15 minutes before classes begin each morning to help students who need special attention. Policy____Regulation____
14. No school board standing committee shall be appointed to perform any of the board's functions. Policy____Regulation____ Neither____
15. No smoking in this room. Policy____Regulation____
16. Appropriate reports will be submitted to the school board on a regular basis to assist board members in carrying out the affairs of the school district. Policy____Regulation____
17. The PTA Council will be granted the use of 3rd Street Elementary School on the second Tuesday of each month without charge. Policy____Regulation____
18. The school buildings within the school district shall be available for citizens to use within the limits of the law and insofar as such usage does not conflict with the instructional programs of the school district. Policy___Regulation____
19. It is the policy of the school district that no outside organization, except the PTA, shall post notices or advertisements anywhere on the school grounds or inside the school. Policy_____ Regulation_____

Quiz Answers: Statements 2, 3, 4, 5, 7, 12, 16, and 18 are policies. Statements 1, 6, 8, 9, 10, 11, 13, 15, 17, and 19 are regulations. Number 14 is a by-law.

The key to answering each entry is to focus on what is to be done or how it is to be accomplished. For example, quiz statement 1 states *how* something is to be done. Therefore, it is a regulation. On the other hand, statement 2 states *what* is to be done. Thus, #2 is a policy. Keep in mind that policies and regulations are closely related, and in some cases, both are included in a statement that is placed in the policy section of the policy manual.

CRITERIA FOR IDENTIFYING A POLICY, REGULATION, OR BY-LAW

A policy is:

1. An assertion of intent/goals
2. Related to a general area of importance
3. Equivalent to legislation
4. Applicable over long periods of time
5. A broad statement that allows for freedom of interpretation and execution
6. Mainly the concern of the school board (or governing body of an organization)
7. A strategy undertaken to solve or ameliorate a problem
8. Concerned with topics of vital interest to the citizenry
9. Related to the question of "What to do?"

An administrative regulation is:

1. Related to a specific problem or area of concern; it is a formula to carry out a policy
2. Mainly the concern of the professional staff (how a policy is to be implemented)
3. A precise statement, calling for exact interpretation and execution
4. Related to the question of "How to do?"

A by-law is:

1. A combination of law and parliamentary procedure

2. Like any other rule in that it specifies required actions, leaving little room for individual judgments
3. A rule that relates to internal board operations
4. Related to the question of how the school board or governing body of an organization will govern itself

HOW EFFECTIVE POLICIES SERVE THE SCHOOL BOARD, THE SCHOOL FACULTY, AND THE SCHOOL DISTRICT'S STAKEHOLDERS

It is true that there are school boards in the nation that resist the adoption of governing policies. There is concern that an approved policy might restrain some actions that the school board wants to implement. In reality, however, a set of effective school policies serves to increase the control of a school board as opposed to restraining it. It must be kept in mind that change is ongoing, and this reality means that organizational policies need to be changed accordingly.

Obstacles to Fulfilling the School Board's Responsibility for Policy Development

There are various reasons why local school boards in all too many school districts do not develop and maintain their own local manual of policies and regulations. A leading reason for not doing so is the *lack of know-how* as related to "what to do." It is common for a new school board member to come into office with some special program idea or ongoing practice that he or she believes needs to be expressed.

In one school district in Kansas, a new school board member telephoned the school superintendent to tell him that he was out shopping for some good deals on vocational education machinery. The superintendent of schools had to direct the board member to the district's school policy and regulation manual relating to business and noninstructional operations commonly included in the section on fiscal management.

On the other hand, poor administrative leadership is missing, and the needed policies within the school district are not brought to the attention of the school board members. Although federal and state requirements bring about the implementation of many school district policies, the local school superintendent most commonly is the leading individual for bringing policy recommendations to the school board. In most cases, the election of some new school board members comes about every four years. This *frequent change of school board members* is another obstacle to the school board's duty of getting effective policies in writing.

The domination of the state's school boards association in most states is ready and willing to sell its membership and policy-making system to local school districts. The lack of staff and/or time is a frequent excuse for a school district not developing its policies and regulations locally. Policy development is difficult; it does take much time. When does it end? The answer is "Never." Change is ongoing, and so is policy change. It is important to keep in mind that policy development is a process and not a project.

In many cases, the lack of staff and/or time, the lack of internal help, or the expenses involved in using consulting services serve as obstacles to local school policy development. However, the attitudes of local school boards toward restrictive policies are among the obstacles for not implementing effective policies. Keep in mind that policy requirements are commonly forced upon local school boards by state and federal agencies.

A Focus on the Benefits of Effective Policies

Effective school policies increase the school board's local control of the school program as opposed to curtailing it. One primary example of policy benefits is vested in the fact that they serve to clarify the work of both the school board and the administrative staff in the school programming process. An understanding of policies and regulations gives insight into the so-called division of labor between the school board and the professional administrative staff.

Local control of education depends greatly on the school district's effectiveness in developing school policies. The school board commonly delegates the responsibility for developing administrative regulations to the school district's professional staff. It is a fact, however, that actions by state and federal authorities pass legislation that requires the local school governing boards to act accordingly. Once again, it must be kept in mind that the state has delegated the authority to develop and implement polices to local school boards.

Norton (2017) points out that developing and/or revising the school district's policies and regulations are major tasks. Policy development is viewed as an ongoing task as opposed to a project. Nevertheless, the benefits of doing so are more than worth the effort needed to accomplish this responsibility. It seems wise to approach the tasks in an orderly fashion and deal with only one section of the policy at a time. Although having a policy manual is not required in all states, having a policy manual and keeping it up to date augers well for the prudent operation of the school district. Formatting and organizing the policy manual so that it is easy to use is of primary importance. Specific strategies for organizing a manual are set forth in detail in chapter 2.

For clarification purposes, consider statements 1 and 2 in the previous quiz. Statement 1, Don't shoot until your see the whites of their eyes, tells us quite specifically when to shoot. It gives an instruction on how to shoot. Regulations serve to answer the question of *how to do* something. Thus, statement 1 is an administration regulation. On the other hand, statement 2 tells us not to shoot until we have a sure shot. It is purposeful in telling us that accuracy is a desired goal. Thus, statement 2 is a policy.

Specific Benefits of Governing Policies and Regulations

Without effective policies, organizational decision making is problematic at best. Several major benefits of organizational policies and regulations are as follows. What is the work of the school board, for example, and how does this work differentiate from the work of the professional staff?

The responsibility of selecting a superintendent is named frequently as a school board's primary role. Although this responsibility is of high importance, we submit that policy development is a school board's primary role. One leading benefit of school policies is that they serve to establish the responsibilities of the school board. Administrative regulations serve to establish the responsibilities of the professional staff.

An understanding of this division of labor in school districts, as well as other businesses and organizations, looms important for meaningful decision making and effective collaborative communication. Major decisions are carried out more efficiently and intelligently when major responsibilities of the governing board and major responsibilities of the staff are known and implemented.

Effective policies serve to establish and implement the important goals and objectives of the organization. Time is saved and energy is fostered by the fact that purposes and activities are more readily communicated and understood. Communication is not only more readily distributed within the organization but also understood more clearly by the organization's clientele. Knowing what purposes loom important in a program activity gives the school superintendent and staff personnel a more intelligent path to follow in deciding best practices. Effective policies serve to give the school board the "legal control" it needs to provide purposeful leadership in directing the school district's educational program.

In local school education governance, policy development is the primary function of the school board. Yet, policy development in education governance commonly gives way to resolving ongoing administrative problems; problems at the local school level which are best left to the local school administrative personnel to resolve. School board policy development and local school district administrative regulations establish the primary differences between a school board and the administrative personnel of the school district. Yet when school boards purchase their policies from outside sources, their actions most often are centered on the administration of the educational practices.

In summary, a policy is a general statement that answers the question of what purposes are important for the school district to accomplish. A policy is general in that it leaves room for the organization's administrative staff and faculty members to set forth the most effective ways for implementing it. What is it that the school district program wants to accomplish? What are its goals and objectives? An effective policy serves to answer these kinds of questions.

An administrative regulation, on the other hand, is more specific. It sets forth the best procedures for implementing a policy. It is more specific and most often generated by the leadership of the administrative staff. Its importance is vested in the fact that it serves to put a policy into action. That is, it answers the question of how to implement the policy.

One important term relating to the school board's governance responsibilities is the term *by-law*. A by-law is a statement that centers on how the school board is going to operate. That is, how is the school board or a board of directors in a business going to govern itself? When will the board meet for official business decisions? What board officers are needed and how will they be selected? What procedures will be in place when the board meets in official sessions? For example, will parliamentary procedures be in place? What constitutes a quorum? Will the board have committees for special work assignments? The topic of by-laws is discussed additionally later in the chapter.

An Example of an Educational Policy That Includes Regulatory Criteria

The following policy example centers on the human resources program and the specific recruitment and selection of personnel. Keep in mind that the terms *section* and *series* are used interchangeably.

The foregoing policy includes criteria that center on both the school district's intended purposes and the purposes of the recruitment and selection process within the school district. The general statement of policy simply states that recruitment and selection are to determine the personnel needs of the school district. The school superintendent's recommendations for hire

SECTION 4000 PERSONNEL

It is the responsibility of the superintendent of schools and persons delegated by him or her to determine the personnel needs of the school district and to locate qualified candidates to recommend for employment to the school board.

There shall be no discrimination in any applicant by reason of race, color, national origin, creed, marital status, sex, or age.

It shall be the duty of the school superintendent to see that persons nominated for employment meet all the qualifications established by law and the school board for the type of position for which the hiring nomination is made. Professional staff, clerical staff, custodial staff, health staff, and all other service positions in the school district are included in the recruitment and selection requirements set forth.

Legal Reference: A.S.A

15.3119 Superintendent and other personnel; qualifications; powers and duties

15,3569 hiring of teachers; contracts. Lafayette School District, South Lafayette

Date of Policy Acceptance:_____

will be ultimately reviewed by school board members. Any discrimination in the hiring process is forbidden. The general policy appears to be applicable for a long period of time. It delegates to the school superintendent certain administrative responsibilities that deal with various purposes of the school board (e.g., discrimination, personnel qualifications, personnel needs).

HOW POLICIES AND REGULATIONS CAN BE DEVELOPED

It has been noted that, first and foremost, in school districts, policy development is a primary responsibility of the local school board. However, as previously noted, school district policies today are most commonly "manufactured" by the state's school boards association. We submit that this procedure is faulty and lessens the organization's communication and control of the school district's program activities.

As underscored previously, local written policies are the primary responsibility of the school board. However, employee groups and parental associations can develop policy proposals as well. It is common for various groups to offer suggestions for needed policies. Such proposals commonly are sent to the school superintendent, who reviews them with other appropriate individuals and groups before submitting them to the school board for official consideration and possible adoption.

How long does it take to develop a set of organizational policies? Policy development is an ongoing task rather than a one-time project. Therefore, the answer to the question "How long will it take to develop the school policies?" is "Forever."

Policies have to be available in writing if effective governance is to prevail. If polices are not available in writing, the governing board is acting on practice. A dominant governing board member might be the one establishing the organization's goals and objectives. The practice of "You vote for mine and I'll vote for yours" is a faulty practice. It seems important to keep in mind that a school board member acting alone has absolutely no authority relative to school governance. However, when acting as a member of a board in session, that member has legal authority for recommending school policies and voting for their adoption. In most states, legal authorities have the right and responsibility of reviewing assessing, evaluating, and approving a school board's policies.

School board education goals are developed through:

1. Cultural sanctions
2. Professional judgments
3. Lay judgment

Policies are developed through:

1. Board action with administrative leadership
2. Local adaptation to goals

Regulations and rules are developed through:

1. Administrative decision making
2. Professional judgments

Policy development is an extremely difficult and time-consuming task. Therefore, it is generally advisable to seek help in developing policies. Such help can suggest strategies to be used, especially if little or nothing has been developed to date. This does not mean that an outside agency establishes the policies for the local school board. There are several strategies that serve to approach policy development. For example, the following steps will serve in a positive way:

1. Review the history of the school board minutes for motions that were implemented which centered on the purposes of the education program.
2. Check on established practices/purposes that have been introduced and implemented. If a school district policy manual has been in place previously, are the statements in the manual policy statements? Does the manual content center on purposes to be achieved? What content is in need of serious review?
3. Examine what other school boards have done (their major policy headlines) but draft your policies in terms of your school district's educational goals and objectives.
4. Consult studies and writings of others in the literature. Understand the content of a policy versus that of an administrative regulation.
5. Enlist the input of others within the school staff. Authorities suggest that all parties affected by the policies should participate in some manner. This principle serves to increase the understanding and acceptance of the policies being implemented.
6. Study groups can be helpful in identifying major purposes.
7. Have other groups review the work completed (PTA, faculty groups, state agencies).
8. Have the school board's legal counsel test the entries for legality.
9. Organize work/review sessions with internal and community groups as fits the case.
10. Establish a review and evaluation of activities following the policy implementation. Are the policy manuals being utilized? Is there a need to rewrite a policy for clarification purposes?
11. How are the school district's policies and regulations being introduced to personnel new to the school district? A school policy commonly should be long-lasting. However, school environments and program practices do change (the COVID-19 pandemic, gender controversy practices, teacher availability, etc.). For example, what criteria loom important in the introduction/teaching of controversial matters and issues regarding teacher, student, and parental rights?

RELATED POLICY AND REGULATION
TERMS AND THEIR IMPORTANCE

Part of the confusion in the use of policies and regulations is vested in the fact that the variety of other terms commonly have some relation to them. Such examples include the terms *legislation, laws, statutes, rules, procedures, standards, orders, codes, ordinances, requirements,* and *directions.* In the following section, each of these terms and other related terms are clarified.

The relationship between and among the following terms used in education and a variety of other businesses and industries is one reason why the law is often confused. We often speak of the law, but various authorities have pointed out that both case law and constitutional law are not laws but the opinions of judges. That is, these "laws" did not go through the legislative process; they were not debated by the representatives of the people and the states.

This fact is not only confusing to the general public but also confusing and misused by the various branches of government due to their misunderstanding of the separation of powers as stipulated in the Constitution of the United States. Separation of powers is the doctrine of constitutional law under the three branches of government: legislative, executive, and judicial. These three branches must operate separately as each one has a distinct and important function to perform. As one education member stated after reading this section, "I don't understand what I don't understand." Perhaps the following discussion will provide a good service.

Clarification of a Few Related and Important Terms

Without question, you have heard and most likely have used each of the following terms used in our everyday affairs. Add some interest to the section which follows by giving your present definition for each term before reading its best definition. For example, you might say to yourself, legislation is what various governing bodies within a state do to carry out an action related to governing practices. Then review the definition set forth in this book for comparative purposes. How close did you come to the appropriate definition?

The term *legislation* is related to law or a body of laws enacted by an official legislative governing body. School courses in social studies and history often include a section on how a bill becomes law. Of course, the answer takes the student through the steps of writing the details of a bill and discusses the steps the bill goes through before it is implemented. The steps are viewed as legislation. The approved end results are viewed as *legislative law.*

An example of legislation: *Public schools within the state and serving students in pre-school, kindergarten, grades 1–6 and 7–12 programs, or any combination of these grading systems, shall have instructional programs for a minimum of 183 days each calendar year.*

The term *law* has been equated with the term *policy*. That is, law commonly is viewed as a policy that is stated in legal terms. In fact, policies are commonly reworded with "stronger" language and set forth additionally as a drafted bill for legislative approval. Laws are less flexible than policies and are far more difficult to change. An education policy might be changed or even dropped by a school board, but a law has been sanctioned by various legal bodies. This fact makes changes in a law much more difficult than changes in a policy.

Laws are developed through a long legislative process. Although education policies are commonly discussed at length by individuals and groups that will be affected by them, the final approval of a policy depends primarily on a single governing group, which is the local board of education. Nevertheless, all local school board policies are subject to state school board approval.

An example of a law: *Education for all Handicapped Children Act of 1973: Requires the state to provide a free, adequate education to all handicapped children.*

A *statute* is a law that has been established by a legislative body. Statutes most commonly are set forth by an upper body of government such as the U.S. Congress. However, statutes are not placed into law unless signed by the nation's president. If the bill is vetoed by the president, the bill does not go into effect unless the veto is overridden by a two-thirds majority of both the U.S. Congress and the Senate.

An example of a statute: *The selling of any alcoholic product to minors by any business is strictly prohibited.*

A statute differs from an ordinance in that an ordinance is local and is passed by a municipal body such as the city council. As noted previously, statutes are laws that are acted upon by legislatures. Federal statutes become law when signed by the U.S. president. If the president does not sign the statute, the veto can be overturned by the Congress with a two-thirds majority vote.

A *standard* is an idea or something used as a model or norm for achievement. It is a model for attainment, such as standards of behavior, performance, and leadership. The state might set forth standards for academic achievement relative to passing from one elementary school grade to the next higher grade. Appropriate behavioral standards commonly are set by the parents of children or by teachers in the classroom. How is the child to act or perform?

An example of a standard: *A minimum score of 65 percent on the state academic achievement test must be earned by every student, among other credit requirements, to receive a high school graduation diploma.*

A *rule*, on the other hand, is a stated requirement governing a conduct or performance activity. It sets forth what can be done or what cannot be done. Closely related "synonyms" are regulation, principle, and requirement. In fact, various references have defined a regulation as a rule within a law that specifies how the ideas of the law are actually going to be implemented.

An example of a rule: *All school visitors must first report their presence when entering the school grounds by reporting first to the central school office.*

An *ordinance* is a local law usually passed by some municipal offices or authorities to regulate the sales of some commodities, such as alcohol and tobacco products, that have implications for public health. Restrictions might be placed, such as age limits for purchasing a product or a curfew on events that tend to be too noisy in residential areas. In most cases, ordinances place monetary or other restrictive penalties on violations of local ordinances.

An example of an ordinance: *Businesses that sell any alcoholic product to the general public must first and foremost be licensed by the state alcoholic control office, including the requirements set forth by state statute #219-A that establishes clock-time limits for selling alcoholic products.*

A *code* is commonly confused with a statute. The primary difference between them is the fact that statutes are designed by the approval of an official state legislative authority, while a code commonly is created by an office or agency and approved later by legislative action. Codes do have the authority of law and are legally enforced. Penalties commonly are attached to code violations, but this practice varies. Codes commonly are related to "how to act" in practice. What principles will be honored for achieving good governance? Codes are established to foster positive governance and are set forth as codes of practice regarding the expected ways to act.

An example of a code: *The selling of any alcoholic beverage to a minor by any business is viewed as a violation of the law.*

The term *order* commonly is used when someone is directed to do something. When used as a noun, however, an individual might receive a written order to appear in court. When used as a verb requiring something to be done, a school principal might order parents to attend a meeting to discuss their son's behavioral problems. Most commonly, perhaps, orders are received by teachers to complete certain tasks, perform certain duties, or complete certain documents. Orders are frequently used synonymously with the term *requirements*.

An example of an order: *All professional faculty members, including administrative personnel, must remain on duty each day until 4:15 p.m.*

unless excused by the member's supervisor or required to be on duty for special assignments as indicated in the member's contract.

The term *requirement* is something that is needed and must be done. It is an act or condition that must be met in order to accomplish a desired end. It is something that is "demanded" or obligatory; it is absolutely necessary. A requirement is something that must be acted upon or achieved in order to meet a desired result.

An example of a requirement: *Each full-time, nontenured teacher in the school system is required to earn 30 units of professional credit during the probationary first three years of their teaching. This requirement ties closely to the concepts of professional development and the attainment of teacher tenure. The school district's manual for professional development sets forth the various kinds of professional activities that can be completed for professional credit.*

The term *procedure* is an established way for doing something, a series of actions that are conducted in a specific manner. Most everyone has been in a meeting when parliamentary procedure was being followed to introduce a practice or to pass a certain proposal. In one sense, a cooking recipe is a procedure for making a certain food product. In the development of policies and regulations, a procedure is common in drafting and implementing a regulation.

An example of a procedure: *Teacher absenteeism: A teacher who is unable to be present to fulfill his or her teaching assignment for the next day is required to meet the following procedures: First, call the absence office (ph. (190) 290-1234) at the earliest possible time. Give your name, school of residence, teaching areas, and any other special instructions.*

If possible and appropriate, give the reason for the absence and the probable time for returning to work. The absence official on duty will inform the school of your absence and will arrange for securing a substitute teacher. The school district policy does not favor half-day absences since securing a substitute teacher for only half a day becomes problematic.

The term *direction* is a guide for doing something or accomplishing a given task. It sets forth the steps that must be taken to meet a desired result. How to fix a broken appliance, reach a certain site, or act in a certain way is specified in the statement of directions. One must follow the directions in order to reach the desired results. In a school situation, behavioral directions might be given to a student by the school principal. Teachers might be given specific directions for supervising the school lunchroom or monitoring the halls during the students' movements from class to class.

An example of a direction: *Weekly lesson plans for each class being taught are to be written using the lesson plan form LP-1009: _____ _____.*

Subject: _____ Topic(s): _____
Presentation/Seatwork: _____
Student Learning Goal(s): _____
Assessment of Student Learning: _____
Student Practice/Homework: _____

A copy of each teacher's lesson plans must be given to the unit chairperson at the beginning of each week of school. Lesson plans will be reviewed by the unit chairperson and returned to the teacher only if recommendations are deemed necessary. Teachers having questions about the lesson plan procedures are most welcome to seek feedback from the unit chair or other appropriate coordinator within the school district. Minor changes in a teacher's lesson plans are most common and expected. Such changes do not have to be reported. However, a teacher's lesson plans are expected to be "in concert" with the school district's curriculum guide for the subject being taught.

SCHOOL POLICIES ARE INITIATED
IN A VARIETY OF WAYS

The educational policies that come to the attention of a school board commonly come in a variety of ways. Several initiators of school policies are as follows:

- The general deliberations of the school board often result in fostering policy needs.
- Recommendations from the school superintendent often lead to new policies.
- Recommendations from the site-based councils often call for policy development.
- Current problems being encountered within the school district tend to bring about policy needs.
- Effective program planning by school leaders at the local level will initiate policy activity.
- Negotiations with teacher and/or support staff associations will initiate policy activity.

- Lay groups and parent/teacher associations point out needs for policy development or revision.
- Federal and state legislative rulings often require statutory policies for schools.
- Court rulings commonly hold implications for required educational policies.
- State and national school board associations commonly recommend policy development. (Norton, 2017)

In addition, major problems facing the nation, such as the COVID-19 pandemic, force the governing boards to give special attention to the effectiveness of current program policies and accompanying administrative regulations. The application of regulations for certain policies in place might be difficult or even impossible to administer. The delivery of instruction, student attendance, virtual learning, teacher responsibilities, health regulations, and other normal practices present the need for revised policies and new program regulations.

DEVELOPING POLICIES AND
CONTROVERSIAL ISSUES

Organizations in the United States are involved in a variety of controversial issues that are prominent in organizations today, and education is no exception. Inequalities in learning opportunities, discrimination in regard to what and how a subject is taught, and the rights of both teachers and students are among the instructional issues facing education.

The questions of how to determine what issues should be included in a classroom discussion, what rights the students and teachers have in regard to teaching certain controversial issues, and how present-day social issues are to be handled in the classroom are among those matters that can be best handled by having purposeful policies that guide the actions of schools/teachers relative to their rights regarding these issues.

The Commission on Professional Rights and Responsibilities set forth four guiding recommendations for the rights of both teachers and pupils in regard to the teaching of controversial issues. In addition, the commission provided an example of a policy statement that established both the purpose and the rights of teachers and pupils on the teaching of controversial issues. The commission's important thinking on this topic is summarized in the following section (National Education Association of the United States, no date).

Example of a Policy Statement

Our policy on the teaching of controversial issues is defined in the terms of rights of pupils rather than in the terms of the rights of teachers. In the study of controversial issues in the public schools, the pupil has four rights to be recognized:

a. The right to study any controversial issue that has political, economic, or social significance and concerning which (at his level) the pupil should begin to have an opinion;
b. The right to have free access to all relevant information including the materials that circulate freely in the community;
c. The right to study under competent instruction in an atmosphere free from bias and prejudice;
d. The right to form and express his own opinions on controversial issues without thereby jeopardizing his relations with teachers or the school.

Examples of Administrative Regulations to Implement Policy

Teachers will use the following criteria for determining the appropriateness of controversial issues for the school:

1. The treatment of the issue in question must be within the range of knowledge, maturity, and competence of the students.
2. The Danske Bank has set forth an excellent example of a group compliance policy. The policy opens with a statement of objectives and then sets forth the definitions, scope, and policy content.

   The group provides a wide range of financial services and products and, as a result, operates in a highly regulated environment. The group assumes its obligations to comply with laws, rules and regulations seriously, including the spirit of the law. This criterion underscores the need for establishing procedures for helping the student to know and understand the information set forth in the students' policy/regulation handbook. Special information sessions for students are to be established.

3. In many schools, a student council is established. Members of this council not only participate in the development of the student policy handbook but also take the responsibility of establishing information sessions on its contents.

4. There should be study materials and other learning aids available from which a reasonable amount of data pertaining to all aspects of the issue may be obtained.
5. The inclusion of the issue should require only as much time as is needed for satisfactory study by the class.
6. The issue should be current, significant, real, and important to the students and the teacher.

KEY CHAPTER IDEAS AND RECOMMENDATIONS

- One basic principle of an effective organization is that its guiding policies must be in written form. If not in written form, the governing board is acting merely on past practices. Unwritten policies tend to change with the ins and outs of changing board membership as opposed to the specific educational purposes of the school district's program.
- Policy development is the primary responsibility of the local school board. Nevertheless, educational policies at the local school district level must be reviewed and approved by the state.
- Policy development is the primary responsibility of the local school board, but it commonly delegates the development of administrative regulations to the local school leaders and faculty members.
- Policy development is an ongoing task rather than a one-time project. In this sense, policy development is ongoing and never completely finished.
- The term *policy* is misused commonly by persons in management positions today, which causes communication problems within the organization.
- The development of a school district's policy and regulation manual by a state's office diminishes the school district's local control. In turn, in many states, school districts tend to have the same governing policies. Locally developed policies serve to increase the concept of local governance control.
- Policies focus on organizational purposes. Therefore, guiding purpose, rather than ongoing practice, is facilitated by having an effective set of governing policies.
- The important question of "What to do?" is answered by an effective set of administrative regulations. The development of administrative regulations looms important in involving the local schools and faculties in the policy development process.
- School policy development is a school board's major strategy for maintaining local control.

- The development of school board policies is delegated to a school board by the state. The school board, in turn, delegates the development of administrative regulations to the local school administration and faculty. Nevertheless, administrative regulations are reviewed and approved by the school board and ultimately by the state authorities.
- Policy and administrative regulation development practices illustrate the division of labor responsibilities of the organization.
- An organization establishes its operational practices by developing a set of by-laws. By-laws set forth the ways in which the organization will govern itself.
- Although school policy might be changed overtime, it is designed as an important purpose that will be in effect for a lengthy period of time.
- How long does it take to develop a set of organizational policies? The general answer is "Forever" since the process is ongoing rather than a one-time project.
- The knowledge regarding the definition of terms such as policy, regulation, by-law, and rule serve to help the communication process. For example, how does a rule differ from an ordinance or a requirement?
- Policies set forth the major purposes that the organization wishes to achieve. How these purposes might be achieved is set forth in the set of administrative regulations that will be developed primarily by the administrative leaders of the school district. Nevertheless, administrative regulations in school district settings must be approved by the local school board and by the state education office.

REFERENCES

Frenzel, B. (2013). *The Missing of Policy Ingredients Amid Dysfunctional Budgeting.* https: //www.forbes.com/sites/billfrenzel/2013/06/26/compromse-the-missing-policy-ingredient-amid-dysfunctional/policy-ingredients-budgeting/?sh=ab6239112c635\

National Education Association of the United States. (No date). Washington, DC. Stock Number 168–04992.

Norton, M. S. (2017). *A Guide for Educational Governance: Effective Leadership for Policy Development.* Lanham, MD: Rowman & Littlefield.

Chapter 2

The Constructs of an
Effective Policy Manual

The primary purpose of this chapter is to set forth systems for codifying policies and regulations that facilitate their placement in the organization's policy manual and their daily utilization by the school district's administration, faculty, and staff and to underscore the importance of policy manuals in other professions, businesses, and industries.

All effective school libraries have a reference system (i.e., Dewey Decimal System) that permits an easy placement of a book on the library shelves and an easy way for anyone to locate the book among the many books in a library. Not having a codification system for referencing library books would be as troublesome as not having a specific home address for each home on the block. The utilization of policy manuals in organizations of all kinds is noteworthy. In this chapter, several examples of policy and regulation manuals are examined. The wide implementation of policy and regulation utilization in organizations nationally is underscored. It might be surprising to learn that professional practices, such as dental care, have comprehensive policies and regulations in place.

We do hear complaints from local school board members that they are losing important local control regarding program provisions and personnel matters. In most cases, these boards are not developing their own policies and regulations. As previously noted, the state school boards association is completing this task for them. In addition, local school administrators, faculty, and classified personnel are not involved in the school district's policy and regulation development and implementation processes.

School districts have two primary systems for coding district policies: the numeric system and the alpha or lettering system. The two foundational coding systems for school policies are the Davies-Brickell System, set forth in 1958, and the National School Boards System established in 1970. In the Davies-Brickell System, a number such as 4231.32 connotes the fourth series or section, the second subseries, the third division, the first subdivision, the third item, and the second subitem of the policy.

The primary series of the Davies-Brickell coding system are as follows:

1000 Community Relations
2000 Administration
3000 Business and Noninstructional Operations
4000 Personnel
5000 Students
6000 Instruction
7000 New Construction
8000 Internal Board Policies
9000 By-Laws

Suppose the school district was using the Davies-Brickell coding system and presently listed the code number 6151.1 in the policy manual. The board members wanted to add *home schooling* to the code as a new item. The new item would change the code number to 6151.2.

The current code 6114 (*Emergencies* subdivision) has six other emergency codes: Fire, 6114.1; Civil Defense, 6114.2; Bomb Threats, 6114.3; Tornadoes and Hurricanes, 6114.4; Enemy Attack, 6114.5; and Inclement Weather, 6114.6. The addition of a new item would include the code 6114.7.

One code in the personnel policy list includes the duties of the school district's *faculty personnel* (4116.31). The subitem #1 represents faculty personnel. Suppose the duties of football, basketball, and track coaches were to be added. How would these codes be entered? For example, the code for the basketball coach could be 4116.32.

THE ALPHA SYSTEM

The Alpha System uses a similar procedure but utilizes letters of the alphabet rather than numbers.

The 12 series in the National School Boards Association (NSBA) Alpha System for a school district are:

A. Foundations
B. School Board Governance and Operations
C. General School Administration
D. Fiscal Management
E. Support Services
F. Faculty Development

G. Personnel
H. Negotiations
I. Instructional Program
J. Students
K. School Community Relations
L. Education Agency Relations

Two examples of the Alpha System follow:

Section B: School Board Policy Manual and Operations

BB School Board Legal Status
BBA School Board Powers and Duties
BBAA Board Member Authority
BBBA Qualifications of School Board Members
BBBB Student Representatives to the School Board

Section G: Personnel

Section G in the National Education Policy Network (NEPN)/NSBA classification system contains policies, regulations, and exhibits on all school employees except the school superintendent, which is located in Section C of the policy manual. Section G is divided into three subsections: A has policies on personnel goals/priority objectives, B has policies on general personnel policies, and C has policies on professional staff. Only A and B are shown in the following personnel policy example.

GA	Personnel Goals/Priority Objectives
GAA	Evaluation of Personnel System
GB	General Personnel Policies
GBA	Open Hiring/Equal Employment Opportunity and Affirmative Action
GBAA	Sexual Discrimination and Harassment
GBAB	Pay Equity
GBB	Staff Involvement in Decision Making
GBC	Staff Compensation
GBCA	Merit/Performance Pay Programs
GBD	Communications with Staff (also BHC)
GBE	Staff Rights and Responsibilities
GBEA	Staff Ethics /Conflict of Interest
GBEB	Staff Conduct
GBEBA	Staff Dress Code

GBEBB	Staff Conduct with Students
GBEBC	Gifts to and Solicitations by Staff
GBEC	Drug Free Work Place (also ADB)
GBED	Tobacco-Free Work Place (also ADC)/Staff No smoking
GBF	Staff Working on Federal/State Grants
GBG	Staff Welfare Protection
GBGA	Staff Health
GBGB	Staff Personnel Security and Safety
GBGC	Employee Assistance/Wellness Programs
GBGD	Workers Compensation
GBH	Staff Participation in Community Activities
GBI	Staff Participation in Political Activities
GBJ	Personal Records and Files
GBJA	Confidential Information and Disclosure of Information
GBJB	Access to Personnel Files
GBK	Staff Concerns/Complaints/Grievances
GBL	Staff Awards and Recognition

The additional major subsections in personnel are Professional Staff (GC) and Support/Classified Staff (GD). If another major subsection, such as Pandemics, was added to the code GBGA, it could be added using code GE.

Section J on Student Policies

The topical student policy listing that follows demonstrates the comprehensiveness of the district's policy planning. Each entry would include the details of the purposes, goals, and objectives of what is to be accomplished in that content area. Keeping such policies up to date necessitates ongoing attention to program changes. It is clear that the policy content is inclusive, because students are a school district's most important reason for a school's existence. Once the specific content of each series is determined, school administrators and other personnel will be certain to save much time and effort in resolving many of the "problems" that they face on a daily basis. The positive results of the student policy series in time will serve the administrative staff and faculty members both time and effort.

JA	Goals and Objectives
JAA	Equal Education Opportunities
JB	Attendance
JBA	Compulsory Attendance Ages
JBB	Entrance Age
JBC	School Admission

JBCA	Resident Students
JBCAA	New Resident Students
JBCB	Nonresidential Students
JBCBA	Tuition
JBCC	Assignment
JBCCA	To Schools
JBCCB	To Classes
JBCD	Transfers and Withdrawals
JBD	Absences and Excuses
JBE	Truancy
JBF	Released Time
JBG	Readmissions
JC	Rights and Responsibilities
JCA	Civil Rights of Minor
JCAA	Due Process
JCAB	Interrogations and Searchers
JCB	Policies and Rules Development (also DCCB)
JCC	Budget Planning Involvement
JCD	Conduct
JCDA	Behavior Code
JCDAA	Smoking
JCDAB	Alcohol Use
JCDAC	Drug Use
JCDB	Dress Code
JCE	Complaints and Grievances
JCEA	Ombudsman
JCEB	Hearing Procedures
JCEC	Demonstrations and Strikes
JD	Discipline
JDA	Corporal Punishment
JDB	Detention
JDC	Probation
JDD	Suspension
JDE	Expulsion

A WORD ABOUT STAFF PERSONNEL AND CLASSIFIED STAFF HANDBOOKS

Almost every school has a student handbook that centers on issues such as student attendance, student behavior, bullying, in-school use of cell phones, and other matters of student activities. How will the school officials deal with such incidents as student fighting, tardiness, bullying, and classroom misbe-havior? How is student suspension to be implemented, and how does it differ from student dismissal? In addition, many school districts have classified personnel policies and student handbooks that set forth policies and regula-tions for practice in these two personnel areas.

For example, a classified staff personnel handbook commonly includes policies and regulations relating to work absences, work benefits, perfor-mance appraisals, payroll, staff conduct, and other operating practices. We note that the "language" of the policy or regulation is not always stated as formally as in the school district's policy manual. In each case, however, the policies set forth in the staff's personnel handbook commonly refer to the school district's policy code. That is, the information in the personnel hand-book on the topic of a drug-free workplace is based on the district's policy that has the code GBEC.

The following example sets forth the absences from work policy com-monly contained in a classified staff personnel handbook:

ABSENCES FROM WORK

ABSENCES (Ref. Policy GDC)

With the exception of Nutritional Services, Transportation, Administration Building, and Custodial Services, when an employee is absent from work, the employee must notify the Substitute Finder Absence Tracking System prior to his/her regularly scheduled start-time. Failure to do so may disqualify the employee from using avail-able leave.

It is the employee's responsibility to comply with his/her depart-ment's absence notification process. Failure to do so may disqualify the employee from using available paid leave or result in disciplin-ary action.

All absences which do not qualify under Board policy (GDBD) are considered unexcused and subject to disciplinary action.

Failure to contact the immediate supervisor or designee for three consecutive days of absence will result in termination of employment.

The district's absence policy continues to set forth purposes on such mat-ters as annual leave, vacations, holidays, sick leave bank, bereavement leave, child care leave, military leave, personal leave, domestic abuse leave, and family and medical leave. Policy information that centers on such "everyday" student matters expedites the resolution of related student problems and lessens the necessary time needed to deal with them. In regard to student policies, it seems reasonable to assume that a student's knowledge of certain consequences serves to lessen their violation.

POLICY MANUALS FOR PROFESSIONAL
SERVICES ORGANIZATIONS

Most people are aware that education and business organizations have policy and regulation manuals in place, but what about other professions and businesses such as physicians, dentists, insurance companies, and banks? In most every profession, policy and procedure manuals are in place. One primary example is the dental profession. DentaQuest (2015) produced a detailed policy and procedure manual. The manual's table of contents includes 10 primary series as follows:

A. Patient Rights
B. Confidentiality
C. Referrals
D. Safety
E. Quality Management
F. Clinic Operations
G. Infection Control
H. Environment of Care
 I. Human Resources
J. Exposure Prevention and Management

Quality management, for example, centers on the purpose of establishing systems and processes within the clinic that will help assure the provision of high-quality oral health care as well as identify any deficiencies in the patient-care processes as opportunities for performance improvement. The following example of a policy on the topic of quality management demonstrates the purposes of quality management in the dentistry profession.

Systems and processes within each clinic will help assure the provision of high-quality oral health care as well as identify any deficiencies in the patient care process as opportunities for performance improvements. Oral health management provisions serve to establish ways and means of evaluating and assessing the outcomes of oral health care provisions that lend to the added quality of the dental outcomes being provided.

An example of a related administrative regulation in the quality management series is as follows:

Three approaches as part of the clinic's Quality Management Program:
- Objective dental record peer reviews to examine and evaluate patient documentation against well-defined criteria. To conduct these reviews, the health center will either staff its own dentists (who will review charts other than their own) or contract with outside dental professionals.
- Objective measures to demonstrate improved health outcomes.
- Subjective patient outcomes assessed via patient satisfaction surveys, which measure the patient's perception of the care experience and results of that care.

The foregoing examples are not set forth to demonstrate what dentists do but to underscore the fact that major professions in practice depend on effective policies and regulations for assuring successful practices. The completeness of the policies and regulations set forth in the DentaQuest manual (2015) is noteworthy. It is a product of the DentaQuest Institute of Westborough, Massachusetts.

THE RECEIPT FOR DETERMINING
BUSINESS POLICY CONTENT

Those readers who have given some thought to the topic of policy development are well aware of its comprehensiveness and complexity. Just one topic, the legal considerations of policy development and implementation, requires detailed legal knowledge. Wall (2020), however, does give thought to what every small business should consider when developing the policies and regulations of the workplace. Such considerations are as follows:

- Employee attendance and paid time off (including accrual or payoff of unused time)
- Sick leave (including the actions to be taken during special problems such as the COVID-19 pandemic)
- Company holidays
- Bereavement leave
- Family and medical leave
- Regular and overtime pay
- Working hours and breaks
- Dress codes
- Rules of conduct

Of course, change is evident and attention must be given to ongoing trends. Remote working practices, discrimination issues, emergency occurrences, social media concerns, and other ongoing problems must be given special attention. Legal compliance requirements loom important as well. It is common for the organization to set forth a policy compliance statement stating that an employee shall comply with all of the company's policies and practices as well as all applicable laws.

POLICIES AND LEGAL REQUIREMENTS

Legal compliance is the process by which a company adheres to the complex rules set forth by policies and processes that regulate business practices in a particular jurisdiction (McMenemy, 2019). The topic of compliance is complex and differs depending on the jurisdiction in which the organization resides. A detailed discussion of legal compliance is beyond the scope of this chapter. However, just how compliance is illustrated within an organization is summarized as follows.

Not only does compliance require being fully aware of the legislation that impacts the organization, but having the ability to show that the organization is in compliance at all times is also required. Is the organization keeping proper financial records, developing and implementing policies in relation to ongoing legislation, and having capable and reliable personnel responsible for assuring that compliance is in place? Lack of compliance can result in serious problems, including reprimands, fines, and loss of confidence on the part of patrons and others who have connections with the organization.

The Department of Health and Human Services recommends several key elements for demonstrating a legal compliance program. An organization that has a legal compliance program has:

- Standards, policies, and regulations in place
- Effective means for screening and evaluating personnel, sales personnel, and other agents
- In-service activities for fostering effective communication and continuous personnel growth and development
- Effective evaluation and assessment strategies related to compliance activities
- Specific methods for dealing with noncompliance activities
- Specific strategies for carrying out improvement measures that are discovered in the organization's program activities

Authorities on the matter of legal compliance commonly recommend that professionals be available for attending to compliance controls, policy development procedures, outcomes, and related policy activities in order to assure that the organization is operating within the legal parameters of the jurisdiction in place. Can every organization afford the costs of operating such a comprehensive and complex program? The answer is that it cannot afford *not* to be in legal compliance. McMenemy (2019) set forth seven steps for evaluating legal compliance, as follows:

Step 1. Know the regulation. What is the company's requirements in regard to the regulation?

Step 2. What are the company's reporting duties? How are the requirements to be reported?

Step 3. Know the company's policies. Are the company's policies up to date and understood by the people in the company?

Step 4. Check the company's records. Are the company's records up to date and easily accessible?

Step 5. Consider related requirements when assessing and evaluating the company's compliance status. What other jurisdictional requirements might have implications for legal compliance such as local licensing codes and legal decisions?

Step 6. Communicate with the company's personnel. Make certain that all company employees are aware of the importance of legal compliance. Are all of the employees well informed about their personal responsibilities in relation to legal compliance?

Step 7. Set up a procedure for conducting important compliance assessments and evaluations. Is what should be happening regarding legal compliance within the organization really happening?

WHY MANY ORGANIZATIONS HAVE TO CLOSE THEIR DOORS

Various factors have been found to be reasons why many organizations must close their doors. Inadequate financing and related problems of the COVID-19 pandemic are two of the leading reasons. However, the lack of planning and poor management loom as important reasons as well. A popular proverb states that an organization's lack of planning is a path toward failure.

Policy development was defined previously as the statements that an organization makes to set forth its primary purposes and what it wants to accomplish. That is, effective policies set forth a plan showing what the organization has achieved in the past, what purposes are presently directing the organization, and what purposes and procedures must be taken to meet future goals and objectives. Group compliance policy, according to Danske Bank, establishes basic principles and standards for managing the compliance risks across the group.

WHAT ABOUT COMPLIANCE POLICY IN SCHOOLS?

The Department of Education has established specific compliance policies for student attendance and participation. Its major sections center on compulsory attendance, attendance strategies, recording attendance, and nonattendance. For example, compulsory attendance policy commonly states that a child who turns six-years-old on or before the 30th of June of the school year is of compulsory school age and must attend school or an approved alternative education program on a full-time basis from the beginning of that school year. Related policies center on attendance strategies, recording attendance, and nonattendance.

Consider the role and responsibilities of the school principal under the policy heading of Attendance and Participation. There are three primary responsibilities of the school principal in this area: (1) being certain that the attendance record of each student in the school is accurately recorded and maintained; (2) being certain that each faculty and staff member in the school is engaged in the school activities that serve to optimize student attendance; and (3) being certain that both faculty and staff personnel understand and are applying the school district's policies and school regulations relative to student attendance and participation.

Without such policy direction, chaos commonly is the result. The foregoing policy requirements demonstrate why it is so important to have staff and faculty personnel participate in policy and regulation development. Such involvement tends to "personalize" the policy and/or administrative regulation. Of course, education is not alone in needing effective policies. An example of policy and regulation development and implementation in organizations other than education is illustrated in the following section.

POLICY EXAMPLES FROM VARIOUS
ORGANIZATIONS/DEPARTMENTS

Policy examples for a variety of organizations and business practices were introduced previously. The purpose of doing so was to emphasize the fact that policy development and implementation support the success of practices in a variety of organizations. The existence of policy development in some practices might be somewhat surprising. The following detailed policy development in the police protection practice is such an example.

THE CINCINNATI POLICE DEPARTMENT

This police department set forth a policy procedural manual to provide an official guide outlining the way to do many of the routine operations which confront the department. A numerical codification system is utilized with the major system titles of: Procedure Manual and Other Binding Written Directives (10.000), Forms Approved for Department Use (11.000), Shift Lineup to Emergency Communication Center (12.000), Field Training Officer Program (13.100), Information Desk (14.105), Citizen Complaints and Reports of Favorable Police Conduct (15.100), Cash Money: Accounting and Security (16.100), Police Records: Storage and Maintenance and Initiation of New Records and Forms (17.100), Civilian Adult School Cross Guards (18.100), and Military Leave (19.103). (Cincinnati Police Department, 2021)

Although the contents of a police manual changes frequently, approximately 175 specific procedures for police operations are in the Cincinnati policy manual. Included in this number of procedures are authorized weapons, reporting police vehicle accidents and damage, use of force, traffic enforcement and vehicle crash reporting. Less well-known police procedures include outside employment, media requests, public appearances, military AWOL arrests, foot pursuits, and many others.

Common Policy Activities of Governing Boards

The Board of Directors' Governance Policy Manual (2021) is an exemplary example of how a governing board can define its purposes and how those purposes are to be carried out. The board identifies three specific purposes of its policy manual: (1) make clear board intent, goals, and aspirations; (2) promote consistency of board action; and (3) clarify board member roles and responsibilities, as appropriate.

One section of the board's policies centers on what the board of directors does. Eight specific areas of responsibility are set forth as follows: A: Budget and Finance; B: Fund Raising; C: Program Evaluation; D: Planning; E: Personnel; F: Board Development; G: Public Relations; and H: Policy. In the policy section, the purposes of policies and procedures are underscored. Members of the board determine the center's policies. Policies can be defined as the broad guidelines that provide a framework for future decision making. Policies are reflected in procedures, which are more specific, narrow parameters that are used in organizational decision making.

Procedures clarify what steps must be taken, what rules must be followed, and who must be included in the process. Procedures are generally formulated by the staff rather than by the board. Organizational policies and procedures are routinely brought to the board for review and approval on a regular basis.

In relation to section E (Personnel), an example of a policy statement is set forth as follows.

Compensation Policy Statement for the Lafayette School District

The policy of the Lafayette School District is to implement a compensation program for personnel that will lead toward the following accomplishments:

1. Attract and retain personnel who are capable of performing effectively in the positions needed in the school district.
2. Contribute to the attainment of district objectives.
3. Be competitive so that the district is able to employ quality personnel in the various teaching, administration, and support areas.
4. Compensate all personnel equitably in proportion to the effectiveness in which they perform the services for which they are employed.
5. Include the compensation factors of salary, benefits, and noneconomical income.
6. Relate salaries and wages to the value of the work for the organization.
7. Gain the acceptance of the school district's publics.
8. Contribute to the economic, social, and psychological satisfaction of the school district's employees.

THE LEADERSHIP ROLE OF AN
ORGANIZATION'S GOVERNING BODY

A successful company or organization requires effective leadership that provides the overall direction and administration for its operations. The governing body serves to interpret the primary purposes of the organization. Such leadership requires several activities, including planning, financial budgeting, personnel supervision, resource allocation, administration, and assessment and evaluation activities. Special attention is given to public relations. Not only are the organization's personnel aware of its community importance, but they are active in ensuring community awareness of the organization's program goals and objectives; community support is essential.

In school districts, the superintendent, in cooperation with the staff and the board, recommends policies for adoption and revision of existing policies (Norton, 2017). However, policies and/or revisions may be proposed by any member of the board, by any lay group or organization, or by any member of the public. Specific policy proposals and suggested amendments to or revisions of existing policies may be submitted to the board in writing prior to a regularly scheduled board meeting. Most commonly, no policy or amendment can be adopted unless it has been discussed in a meeting prior to adoption, unless a majority of the board has voted otherwise.

In some school districts, a school board member serves as the chairperson of a committee in one area of program importance. That is, a board member leads a committee that deals with a school program such as community relations, curriculum development, athletics, or other educational program areas. A committee serves to assess, evaluate, and recommend improvements in the assigned program area and recommends policies related to that area. The committee strategy is "believed" to give more in-depth attention to an important school program area.

Special committees commonly include representative board members, teachers, parents, and perhaps a representative student. Procedurally, committees report their recommendations to the school superintendent rather than presenting them directly to the school board. It should be noted, however, that not all school boards favor such special committees.

One school board member was asked about the matter of school board committees. That is, why do some school boards have special committees and others do not? This board member noted that the size of the school district is one reason why special committees are in favor. The school board finds it difficult to handle so many different areas of the school's program operations. In addition, she also noted that school boards commonly operate in a political atmosphere.

Politics can become a problem. In some cases, conditions such as the opening of schools, integration, sex education, the wearing of masks by teachers and students due to COVID-19, the reluctance of teachers to return to the classroom, and other curricular offerings weigh heavily on school operations.

Can an Effective School Board Member Be Identified?

The Great Boards Organization (2018) set forth "5 Essential Qualities of an Effective Board Member," as follows:

1. Dedicated and committed, including an unwavering interest to achieve the goals of the organization
2. Able to lead and influence others
3. Straightforward and impartial
4. Knowledgeable and insatiable learner
5. Values discretion and confidentiality

Quality 1 above centers on the school board's primary purposes, as these characteristics would be set forth in its adopted policies.

The Center for Public Education (Dervarics & O'Brien, 2019) set forth eight characteristics of effective school boards. One of the criteria states that effective school boards are accountability driven. That is, effective school boards spend less time on operational issues that are to be carried out by the administrative staff. More time is focused on policies that center on the importance of improving student achievement. Such policies serve to answer the following questions: Why do our schools exist? Whom do we serve? What do we want our school programs to achieve? How best can these programs be achieved?

A Policy and Regulation Exercise

Directions: For each statement, one through five, in an organization's policy manual, insert a viable *administrative regulation* that serves to determine how the policy is to be implemented. The following example illustrates a specific policy and follows with an example of one relational administrative regulation.

Example: Policy: Membership in the university program places a special obligation on all students to participate responsibly to a safe and positive learning environment. This obligation implies the responsibility of each member of the student body to maintain an environment in which behavior of any individual is not disruptive.

Example: Administrative Regulation: It is the responsibility of each faculty member to enforce and maintain the standards of behavior acceptable to preserving positive atmosphere for effective teaching and learning in accordance with requirements of the course syllabus.

Exercise

1. Policy: Safe working and learning conditions are of primary importance at Lafayette University. Prevention of discrimination on the basis of sex, race, color, age, national origin, religion, disability, or harassment is to be prevented in all programs and activities provided or sponsored programmatically.

   Administrative Regulation:

2. Policy: Appropriate evaluations of student performance serve to provide the student's ongoing status in relation to the required expectations of a specific course.

   Administrative Regulation:

3. Policy: School principals are responsible for establishing procedures for student control.

   Administrative Regulation:

4. Policy: Employee reemployment is subject to district need and to requirements that may not be set forth by state statutes.

   Administrative Regulation:

5. School administrative personnel and qualified nurses within the school shall be responsible for verifying the registration status and ongoing authorization concerning the medical use of marijuana for any student.

   Administrative Regulation:

LOCAL CONTROL OF EDUCATION

In chapter 1, it was pointed out that effective school district policy planning, development, and implementation serve to retain the local school control of the educational program. Both federal and state mandates for local school operations have been in practice historically. However, when local school boards take the initiative for policy development, local control is enhanced.

Kirst (1991) points out that school boards can only become stronger when they have strong support among the American public. In an early study of the status of school boards, the public viewed school boards as serving to maintain a close relationship with the citizenry. However, conditions change and the events of the pandemic, including open or closed schools, the wearing of masks or no masks, and the teaching of certain controversial topics, such as sex education and various philosophies of organizational governance, have served to divide personal thoughts relative to school program content and teaching practices.

POLICY AND THE TEACHER WORKLOAD PROBLEM, WITH A SMILE ON ONE'S FACE

In the most recent discussions regarding needed changes in education, the wearing of masks, free tuition for some students, open or closed school options, teacher workload, and doing something about education for immigrants have dominated discussions on education. Just what must be done to solve the major problem of teacher loss in educational practices remains unresolved. Historically, as previously noted, education loses 15 to 25 percent of those teachers who completed only one year in the profession. Recommendations for dealing with this major problem is discussed in depth in chapter 3. A recent book, *Teacher Workload* (Norton, 2021), centers on the needed solutions for helping to resolve the teacher workload problem.

With a smile and some humor in mind, Norton (2021) commented on how to solve the problem of teacher work overload that includes some suggestions found in the literature. For example, don't aim for perfection, just do the job as you have been doing it; ask for help and learn to say "no"; when things get out of control, get them under control; remember the phrase, "It is what it is" and use it often; list your priorities according to their difficulty, and then do the easiest ones first; call in sick; if you find yourself working too many hours, just work fewer hours; when the principal says, "Think of your students," just think of the ones that give you all those dxxx problems; when the school superintendent asks every teacher to give just 10 percent more, just ask him or her if that figure can be applied to your salary increase next year; and lastly, if you just fail to accomplish all the work that is piled on your desk, remember that a person can learn a great deal through his or her failures.

THE SCHOOL PRINCIPAL'S LEADERSHIP

School district policies are adopted by the school board and implemented by the school district's administrative staff and local school principals. Being fully aware of the policies set forth by the school board is of primary importance. School principals can serve the policy function of their school districts in various ways, including working with their instructional and service staffs in understanding the important goals and objectives that have been set forth by the school board. Other ways in which the principal can promote effective school district policy practices include:

1. Holding discussion sessions with teachers, students, and parents that focus on answering such questions as: What is our primary purpose? Whom do we serve? Why do we exist? How best can we achieve our purposes?
2. Implementing school programs and activities that best serve the achievement of the school district's stated purposes as set forth in district school policy. What must we do to have the ability to achieve our stated purposes?
3. Centering on what can be done to improve the learning climate for students.
4. Implementing assessments and evaluations that loom important for determining the status of school policy implementation.
5. Understanding the leadership necessary for implementing the school district policies at the school level.
6. Understanding that a school district is a system, and a system requires cooperative relationships and collaborative program development and implementation.

A FOCUS ON STUDENT POLICIES

The literature on school policies for students commonly focuses on student conduct/discipline, attendance, dress code, bullying, cell phone use, search and seizure, tardiness, and suspension and dismissal. An example of each of these areas is set forth as follows.

Student Policy on Conduct and Discipline

Although student conduct and discipline are related, they do differ. Student conduct focuses on the school's expectations as to how the student must act and what they must do to maximize their learning potential. On the other hand, student discipline centers on behavioral expectations and the consequences of not doing so. The terms *student suspension* and *student expulsion* are commonly set forth in detail in a school district's policy manual. The suspension of a student from attending school is generally defined as a time of no more than 10 days and can be sanctioned by the school principal. *Student expulsion,* on the other hand, is much different and commonly requires a formal student hearing.

The following information describes the common procedures related to a student expulsion hearing. It is understood that such hearings do differ among the states.

Student Hearing Procedures

A qualified and impartial hearing officer is appointed after all appropriate persons are identified and informed that such a hearing is to be scheduled. School officials prepare in writing the details related to the student's case.

The hearing is held. The presiding officer opens the hearing by noting the time and place of the hearing. Attendees at the hearing are introduced. Copies of the certified mailings regarding the notification of all persons along with rights and procedures of the hearing are reviewed.

The reasons for the student hearing are set forth and the related facts of the hearing, such as time information, violations of school policies/regulations, accusations, and legal truths are underscored. Additional related information is recorded, including: current school principal and student experience and primary responsibilities; safety of school environment; pupil enrollment and welfare responsibilities of school authorities; understandings of student behaviors; review of state's statutes related to the specific violations; school's expulsion policies; letters to parents by certified mail; telephone calls; the student's discipline file; student's violations of school policies; records of student behaviors; student attendance record; handbook for student's information; off-campus student behavior; student's awareness of school policies on discipline and behavior; and on- and off-campus student violations.

Student's *understanding* of school policies on conduct and violations is examined. The information in the student policy handbook is considered. Exhibits of the student's violations of school rules and examples of disorderly conduct in the school settings are presented. Out-of-school violations are presented as well. Student handbook information and teachers' records of the student's absenteeism, attitudes toward school, records of apathy, and disregard by student of school faculty and administration personnel counseling are reviewed.

The hearing officer completes a comprehensive written report of the hearing that is sent to the school district's board of education that rules on the case.

KEY CHAPTER IDEAS AND RECOMMENDATIONS

- Local school district development of its policy and regulation manual serves to strengthen the concept of local school control.
- Policy manuals are valuable instruments for the successful operation of the educational organizations but serve successfully in business and industrial organizations as well.
- Policies answer the question of what is to be accomplished in an organization, and regulations answer the question of how those purposes are to be accomplished.
- Only the local school board has the authority to adopt policies for the school district. However, the state board of education or another official state body must approve any and all local school policies.
- Many school districts nationally do not develop their own policy manuals. Rather, they purchase this service from their state's administrative organization. Thus, faculty personnel are not directly involved in the policy process. The result is the fact that the faculty members have no "personal relationship" with the policy results.
- Two of the primary policy codification systems utilized for policy and regulation development are the Davies-Brickell numerical system and the Alpha System that uses letters rather than numbers to identify each entry.

REFERENCES

Cincinnati Police Department. (2021). *Police Department Procedural Manual.* Cincinnati, OH.

Davies, D. R., and H. M. Brickell (1958). *An Instructional Handbook on How to Develop School Board Policies, By-Laws, and Administrative Regulations.* Naco, AZ: Daniel R. Davies.

DentaQuest. (2015). *Board Governance Manual.* Westborough, MA: DentaQuest Institute. dentaquestinstitute.org.

Dervarics, C., and E. O'Brien. (2019). *Eight Characteristics of Effective School Boards.* Alexandria, VA: Center for Public Education/National School Boards Association.

Great Boards Organization. (2018). *5 Essential Qualities of an Effective Board Member.* https://greatboards.org/5-essential-qualities-of-an-effective-board-member/.

Kirst, M. K. (1991). "School Board: Evolution of an American Institution." *The American School Board Journal, 178*(11), A11–A14.

McMenemy, L. (2019). *What Is Legal Compliance?* Diligent Insights. https://www
.diligent.com/insights/legal-compliance/steps-evaluating-legal-compliance/.

Norton, M. S. (2017). *How School Boards Govern Themselves: A Guide for
Educational Policy Governance.* Lanham, MD: Rowman & Littlefield.

Norton, M. S. (2021). *Teacher Workload: Primary Recommendations for Improvement.*
Lanham, MD: Rowman & Littlefield.

Wall, S. (2020). *10 Company Policies Every Small Business Should Consider.*
HRDirect website. https://www.hrdirect.com/policies-for-small-businesses.

Chapter 3

Policy Implementation in Organizations

The primary goal of this chapter is to set forth the details of policy and regulation development that pertain to the responsibilities in all organizations, including local public and private school boards.

Policy development is viewed as the primary function of a local school district's board of education. Such authority is delegated to the local school board by the state's school board or another governmental agency within the state. Although the development of local school district administrative regulations is delegated to local boards, this task is commonly developed by the school district's administrative personnel and approved by the local school board. This procedure, however, is generally aborted when the local board just purchases its policy manual from the state's administrators' association.

In any case, policy development and implementation take place within the culture and climate of the organization. These characteristics commonly differ within communities in general and even within the various school districts in a community. This chapter, therefore, gives special attention to the characteristics of that culture and climate. This emphasis underscores the advice commonly given to education leaders and other leaders of organizations: Know Your Community.

This chapter centers on the important processes for putting organizational policies and regulations to work. Just how can an organization promote its efforts to be more effective and efficient? Knowing the organization's purposes and having directions for accomplishing them are of primary importance. In the case of school districts, the school board acts in behalf of the state at the local school level. In practice, the state's responsibilities are delegated to the local school districts. In most cases, the state has given school boards the autonomy to set forth policies and regulations that meet local school purposes and needs. Local school boards are in the best position to be able to know the community. Ultimately, the purposes and needs are set forth in the school district's policy manual.

QUALIFICATIONS FOR SCHOOL BOARD MEMBERSHIP

The qualifications for school board membership are limited at best. In most states, school board candidates must be a registered voter in the state and have been a resident of the school district for a minimum of one year preceding the date of election. In addition, most states require that a school board candidate hold at least a high school diploma or its equivalent, be at least 18 years of age, not be a school trustee or related to an employee of the school district, and not have a criminal record.

We submit that the foregoing list of school board member requirements is insufficient for meeting the job responsibilities of an effective school board member. A school board member must be prepared to deal with the educational as well as the legal program issues that face all school boards.

Education is viewed by a large majority of America's population as being high on the list of America's primary priorities. We submit that qualifications for serving on local school district governing boards should require appropriate qualifications for such service.

SCHOOL BOARD POLICY MAKING

If a school board is to fulfill its primary responsibilities of governing the school district, it is vital that the board has an ongoing process for developing, implementing, and assessing its purposes and practices. Important questions to ask include: What are our primary purposes? Whom do we serve? How best can we meet our purposes? How can we assess and evaluate our purposes? How best can we inform our faculty personnel and stakeholders about our purposes? We contend that a primary answer to such questions is vested in the school board's statement of purposes: its policies and regulations.

There are many sources that hold implications for needed educational policy. The following list sets forth several such sources:

- Matters of importance currently faced by the school board commonly point to policy needs and effective administrative regulations for their local school implementation.
- The ongoing issues facing the school board commonly hold implications for the development of guiding policies.
- Faculty relationships often result in purposeful policies that set forth positive goals and objectives to be achieved in practice.

- School board and faculty negotiations often result in the initiation of new policies relative to board and personnel relationships.
- School boards that have special program committees often receive feedback for needed policies on specific program operations.
- The school superintendent's recommendations commonly result in new board policies and/or administrative regulations.
- Teacher associations and related school program relationships are the basis for many school district polices related to program provisions, student/teacher relationships, and parental involvement in school matters.
- State and federal regulations relating to local school education weigh heavily on a school district's program practices.
- National crises, such as the COVID-19 virus and other troublesome conditions, bear upon school matters that tend to result in policy changes.

THE LANGUAGE OF SCHOOL
POLICIES AND REGULATIONS

Norton (2008) points out that the language of written policies and regulations is of primary importance. Attention to the language of written policies can obviate many problems of interpretation and possible conflict. Because a variety of publics utilize policies and regulations, they must be readable and meaningful to all concerned. Poorly written, ambiguous policies tend to confuse rather than inform. Furthermore, because policies serve as legal extensions of the school board, precise language that is presented in a clear, straightforward manner is of paramount importance. In policy writing, the statement, "You get what you write," is a basic truth.

Consider the following human resources policy statement for personnel:

In order to provide fairness among all support personnel, payment for overtime services will be based on a payment of $12 to $18 per hour depending on the nature and difficulty of the work assignment. Overtime work should be fairly assigned by the principal of the school in which the work is to be done. Overtime assignments should be equally divided among the school's faculty and support personnel.

The policy statement might appear to be clear on the surface, but certain language is questionable and must be raised. For instance:

1. Just how is the difficulty of the work to be determined?
2. How can the fairness of work quality be determined for any specific job by principals throughout the school system?
3. Are all school principals qualified to determine the payment policy for the various job assignments of both faculty and support personnel?

4. What jobs are to be paid $12 per hour and what jobs are to be paid more?
5. Is the teacher's preparation work at home to be considered for overtime pay?
6. What work is considered to be eligible for overtime?
7. How is overtime work to be identified?

Positive language always is recommended in policy and regulation writing.

Negative wording: As part of the teacher's work responsibilities, every teacher is required to stand outside the door of their classroom, while students are moving from classroom to classroom, for the purpose of controlling student behavior or minding other problems that are certain to occur.

Positive wording: In order to facilitate the movement of students within the hallways of the school, teachers can be most helpful by standing outside their classroom door when students are moving from classroom to classroom.

THE IMPORTANCE OF LEGAL COMPLIANCE

McMenemy (2021) underscores the vital importance of adhering to the complex policies and processes that regulate practices in various organizations. Knowing and understanding the legislation that is set forth by the state's organizational board, along with being able to show that the organization's practices are in compliance with such legislation, is essential. Failure to do so can lead to legal actions that result in court rulings and reputational damage that undermine the organization's stated purposes and reputation.

Compliance refers to the duty of the organization to obey the law and to take steps to be in compliance with it. When the organization is well aware of the policies, rules, and procedures that are set forth by the legislative body, and is able to show compliance practices, *responsible compliance* is in evidence. Failure to do so can result in serious problems for the organization. Questions to be answered by the organization include:

1. What are the *regulations* applicable to the organization, and what is required of your organization in relation to them?
2. What are the *reporting requirements* set forth in the regulations applicable to the organization's regulations?
3. Are the legal *compliance policies* that are put in place up to date and being adhered to?

4. Are the records of all *compliance activities* being properly completed and checked on a regular basis?

DO SCHOOL DISCIPLINE POLICIES
SUPPORT STUDENT LEARNING?

According to the National Association of School Psychologists (NASP, 2018), "Effective school discipline policies are critical to promoting students' successful learning and well-being" (p. 1). For example, effective discipline policies serve to strengthen students' behavioral skills by focusing on their behaviors while preserving the integrity of the learning environment.

However, negative approaches to discipline have not been successful. For example, turning student misbehavior cases over to external justice systems has not been effective in reducing student behavior problems. As underscored by the National Association of School Psychologists (NASP, 2018), punitive discipline methods tend to place these matters in the hands of external systems. This procedure tends to "criminalize" student discipline measures which are best handled by school officials such as trained guidance counselors, health personnel, and trained administrative personnel.

NASP (2018) underscores the fact that effective school discipline policies serve to strengthen students' behavior skills by: identifying and attending to the specific causes of a student's misbehavior; improving the climate in which the misbehavior is taking place, helping to ensure the dignity of all school personnel by implementing positive approaches to disciplinary measures; and by improving present disciplinary procedures.

How might these principles be enacted? First and foremost, the organization's policies must be tailored to its purposes, needs, and structure. For example, a policy must be structured so that the recipients of the policy are able to carry it out. If a policy is structured so as to be too difficult to be carried out by the people for which it is intended, it is evident that its life will be short. This principle serves to underscore the importance of involving the recipients in the planning and implementation processes.

A plan that involves the members of the organization must be established. A policy is not something that is to be set upon the personnel. Rather, the organization's personnel must be involved in both the development and implementation of the policy. If such participation is not in order, the completed policy manual is bound to be found just sitting and gathering dust on the shelves of the organization's personnel.

A common problem faced by policy makers is that of drafting policies that conflict with employment law or other legal requirements. Introductory policy statements should be reviewed by the organization's legal counsel or other authoritative legal counsel. In fact, rather than wait until a policy or policy manual is completed, it is wise to have the organization's legal representative make certain that the policy(s) complies with all regulatory requirements before it is put into practice. Paying attention to the outcomes of court actions on educational matters is highly recommended. Such court actions have implications for developing new policies as well as for correcting ongoing policies that conflict with current legal court rulings.

THE PRIMARY IMPORTANCE OF
ORGANIZATIONAL CULTURE AND CLIMATE

It seems clear that successful policy development and implementation are influenced by the factors of organizational culture and organizational climate. The following section considers the characteristics of climate and culture and their relationships with policy making. There is no question that the climate and culture of schools and school districts differ. This fact supports the conclusion that "purchased" state-developed policies that are distributed to all schools is a futile provision. If indeed school districts, schools, and students differ substantially, a copy of the canned state-developed policy manual for schools should not be appropriate.

Unfortunately, local school districts commonly are happy to receive the state's version of a school district's policy manual. After all, policy development is a difficult process at best. When is the task of policy development completed? The answer is "Never." Policy development is ongoing; outdatedness, educational changes, official legislation, and court rulings affect "current" educational policies on a continuous basis. In addition, school board members, teachers, and practicing school administrators most often have had little or no instruction on policy and regulation development. Thus, as pointed out in chapter 1, important terms such as policy, regulations, rules, and laws are commonly misused. A school principal might say, "Our school *policy* is 'no smoking anywhere in the school or on the school grounds.'" In this case the word *policy* should be replaced by the word *rule*.

Organizational Culture and Climate

We contend that policy development is affected directly by the culture and climate of the organization in which it is developed. *Culture* is the set of important beliefs and values that members of an organization share. *Climate*, on the other hand, is the collective personality of an organization. It is the atmosphere that prevails as characterized by the social and professional interactions of people.

Culture is more normative than climate in the sense that it is a reflection of the shared values, beliefs, and underlying assumptions of members across an array of organizational dimensions that include but go beyond interpersonal relationships. Climate is more personal in tone and substance than culture. It is revealed in the attitudes and behaviors of members both in the organization and the community. The importance of these phenomena is vested in their importance of effecting organizational policy and regulation development.

Thus, when an organization's culture is observed, the evolved form of social practice that has been influenced by many complex interactions between people, events, situations, and general circumstances, is always evolving. It can be seen as having a discernible effect on cooperation, competition, equality or dominance, and consciousness and concerns. Each of these characteristics is reflected in the opinions relative to beliefs as to what is important and what needs to be established as an important purpose to be carried out in an organization and the community at large. Such results most commonly lead toward the development of an organizational policy and its implementation.

The significance of organizational culture for an organization has been succinctly underlined by Schein (2010). As he stated, "The bottom line for leaders is that if they do not become conscious of the cultures in which they are embedded, those cultures will manage them. Cultural understanding is desirable for all of us, but it is essential to leaders if they are to lead" (p. 1).

The various definitions of culture do vary. Previously, culture was defined as the set of important beliefs and values that members of an organization share. On the other hand, Pai and Adler (2001) defined culture as the whole of humanity's intellectual, social, technological, political, economic, moral, religious, and aesthetic accomplishments. Rich's similar definition states that "culture is a pattern of human behavior, including thought, speech, and action, shared by a group of people." Lorch believes that culture is the beliefs that top managers in a company share about how they should manage themselves and other employees. Several others have expressed the concept that culture is an expression of people's deepest needs.

In any case, each definition of the term *culture* suggests the characteristics of purpose and its implementation. As such, it underscores the importance of policies and regulations in organizational practice.

A positive climate sets the tone for the human behaviors necessary for achieving organizational success. It is supportive of effective policy development. A healthy organizational climate serves to stimulate members' best efforts toward implementing the stated administrative regulations required for fulfilling the stated policies that have been set forth as purposes to be achieved.

Effective human relationships require a climate of trust, mutual respect, and clarity of function. Such conditions are inhibited in organizations where distrust and poor human relations exist. A positive organizational climate encourages innovative practices and facilitates changes that commonly are required when new policies are implemented. When organizational leaders are attempting to achieve creative change, they should first examine the organizational climate, and if it is less than favorable, take the necessary steps required to change it. Thus, attention to school climate is of paramount importance because it affects all of the important reasons why an organization can reach its stated goals successfully.

How Can Organizational Climate Be Determined?

One school principal was asked just how the climate of a school could be determined. Reportedly, she responded that one just had to go into the school, visit the school office and its personnel, visit two or three classrooms, visit the teachers' lounge, and observe the happenings that take place when students move from classroom to classroom. Perhaps a much more objective proce-dure would be to implement one of the more "scientific" procedures that do provide a much better picture of a school's health.

Nearly 60 years ago, Halpin and Croft (1963) set forth the Organizational Climate Description Questionnaire (OCDQ). This instrument has been used in hundreds of schools to determine the state of the climate in school settings. The OCDQ is completed by the teaching staff of the school and yields mean scores for eight subtests related to teacher and principal behavior. The six climate types are arranged on a general continuum from *open* to *closed.* The open climate, for example, often is described as one in which members enjoy friendly relationships, and possess the incentive to work things out to keep the organization moving.

The Purdue Teacher Opinionnaire (PTO) (Bentley & Rempel, 1970) and the High School Characteristics Index (HSCI) (Stern, 1964) are other instru-ments which can serve school personnel in assessing climate. The PTO provides results on rapport among teachers, teacher status, and other climate indicators which can be compared to national norms. The HSCI is a standard-ized instrument with 30 scales which relate to seven factors of school climate. It differs from other climate instruments in that it assesses school climate from the students' perspectives.

While the foregoing climate considerations do provide suggestions for improving climate in schools, the need related to this topic is to underscore the value of developing effective policies and regulations in an environment that facilitates positive and effective organizational policies and regulations. School personnel do well when they focus on such questions as: Who are we, what are our purposes, and how best can we carry them out? Effective policies and administrative regulations serve to answer such questions.

KNOWING YOUR COMMUNITY

The statement, "Know Your Community," is one often repeated in education. Whether the phrase is expressed in connection with public relations, administrative functions, or perhaps in a more specific instructional context, the implication is that knowing the make-up of the community, its various publics, it power structure, its customs and traditions, its hopes, and its history is essential for teaching, administration, and related educational programs in a particular community. We submit that knowing your community is an absolute essential for developing and implementing effective policies in an organization.

All too often, the responsibility of an organizational leader for learning about the community is taken lightly or simply left to chance. The learning procedure in all too many instances is a passive one and depends largely on incidental day-by-day and year-by-year personal activities and contacts. Certainly, gaining insight into the make-up of a community or organization is a continuous task. However, leaders of an organization might find the following "10 easy lessons" of special value to an organizational leader for learning a great deal about their community in a relatively short time period (Norton, 1968).

The following chapter discussion centers on education, school districts, and their personnel. Nevertheless, the "lesson learning procedures" set forth for school leaders, have implications for organizational leaders in all public and private enterprises.

A Four-Hour Learning Lesson—10 Suggestions for Learning about the Community

1. *Have a special talk with the organization's board of directors.* People who serve on boards of education and other boards of directors consist of members who represent several different aspects of the community. Organization leaders should ask for a special session with the board members to discuss the topic of community relations. Ask members specific questions that may not have been appropriate in the interview prior to your appointment. You will gain some valuable information regarding the characteristics, customs, and traditions of the community. In turn, the board will be happy to know of your interest in this area of your work.

2. *Confer with the local manager of the Chamber of Commerce or a prominent local business manager.* These individuals will have had many contacts with a variety of "publics" of the community. They will know the names of the leaders of various community programs and offices. They are likely to know something about the power structure within the community that "controls" certain aspects of the political world.

3. *Arrange to see the mayor or another city official such as the city manager or a city council member.* These community leaders have a close touch with the community pulse on matters related to both financial measures and policy matters.

4. *Visit with the president of the local ministerial association.* The minister's work calls for a close relationship with the community members, who include many of the same personnel with whom you will associate. This individual will have had a close relationship with the people in the community.

5. *Arrange to visit with the editor(s) of the local newspaper.* Newspaper staffs are commonly much alert to the make-up of the community. Newspaper editors are likely to be most alert to the make-up of the community. Thus, they are likely to be close to the real community issues and concerns.

6. *Ask your secretary to arrange a meeting with your chief administrative staff.* Attempt to gain their viewpoints on the "publics" which they encounter in the fulfillment of their duties. What matters and issues appear to be of most importance to the individuals whom they encounter in their work?

7. *Arrange to have morning coffee with the presidents of local civic clubs.* These people are most likely to be a prominent community leader in their own right. Positive relationships with these leaders will pay dividends for gaining important feedback on issues that arise that have implications for the organizations that you represent.

8. *Ask the PTA Council for 30 minutes at their next meeting.* Place an emphasis on gaining their view of the community and their importance in serving to meet the important goals and objectives of the local school program.

9. *Arrange to meet with the local teachers' and administrators' organizations to discuss the topic of community relations.* Keep the focus on why schools exist and whom they serve. Why do schools exist? Why are the members of these professional associations so important in serving to develop important school policies and implementing the necessary administrative regulations?

10. *Determine other groups, agencies, and individuals that should be contacted.* If you are a school leader, don't overlook your own school members and groups. When we say Know Your Community, the closest

communities of school leaders are teachers, parents, and students. How are you going to underscore their importance in the policy and regulation decisions that must be made in any successful organization? What is learned by your visits with your community's membership can serve to help you establish goals that are important for the organization's success.

OH HUM, NOT MORE TALK ABOUT
THE PLANNING PROCESS

Yes, effective planning is the sine qua non of organizational success. Effective planning serves in helping the organization determine what it wants to be and what it needs to do to achieve those purposes. First and foremost, planning serves to clarify the objectives of an organization. It helps in identifying what the organization has to do to ascertain the resources for accomplishing the desired ends and gaining the needed financial support required by the task.

What kinds of things must be done? Forecasting personnel needs is one essential consideration. This task includes projecting program enrollments, assessing labor markets, completing inventory assessments of needed materials and equipment, and conducting a position analysis that assesses the personnel needs and the implementation of certain strategies such as the Markovian analysis for forecasting employee supply. What alternatives are available if the personnel market is found to be unfavorable?

At the time of this writing, COVID-19 was active. Personal illness and frequent death were present. Education was troubled. New teachers were limited, and hundreds of the licensed teachers were deciding to refrain from further practice. Home schooling was losing favor due to the fact that students were falling behind in their learning. If this was not enough, the market was depressed, and "fear" of a nationwide depression was on the minds of the nation's people.

HELPFUL RECOMMENDATIONS? WHAT
ARE THE SCHOOLS TO DO?

Financial support for education was a limited priority. Governmental funds were being generously provided for helping the defense of the country of Ukraine from Russian invasion. Individuals in America differed on the question of what to do. Private schools were abundant for students whose families had the financial means to enroll in those programs. Should we give education the full financial support it needs, or should we use financial resources for funding Ukraine's war with Russia?

At the time of this writing, the best answers to the foregoing questions were not clear, but supporting the Ukrainian war effort appeared to be a priority. Inflation was rampant. Gasoline was nearing $6.00 a gallon. In short, the quality status of education in the United States for students was unclear. The quality of education seemed to vary from poor to good across the United States. Private schools were abundant for students whose families had the financial means to enroll in those programs. In many cases, unlicensed personnel were in public school classrooms as teachers.

SECURITY RISKS AT SCHOOLS

An article in the *Arizona Republic* newspaper (Kunichoff, 2022) addressed the safety problems of one school principal in Arizona. The school principal noted the changes that had taken place since he first assumed the leadership of his school. Two decades ago, the principal loved the big glass doors of the school building that let in streams of sunlight into the halls of the school. But now, those doors were seen as security risks since they made it easy to see inside the school and difficult to secure. Although efforts had been made to improve school security, funds have been difficult and/or impossible to come by.

What curriculum was being taught and how well students were learning varied widely. It wasn't a matter of just putting safety into place, but what should be done to safeguard students and faculty personnel. How was safety to be accomplished in schools all across the nation?

Many new safety measures were recommended and even installed in some school settings. Examples of such recommendations included: putting more police or safety patrols in every school and giving teachers firearms for protection purposes. Consider the teachers that you had in elementary and secondary schools. Were any of them viewed as being capable of handling a firearm for protection?

Other *recommended* safety recommendations included having safety monitors at each school door to check on who was coming into the school and to examine what each person was carrying. School doors were to be locked at all times. Safety drills were to be conducted in every school. Some schools initiated a rule that no visitors were to be allowed in any school during school hours. Student absences were to be carefully checked every day. Where was the absent student, and what was he or she doing?

What a sad commentary for a learning facility that has historically been viewed as a safe environment where children went to play and learn. Private schools were abundant in some school districts for students whose families had the financial means to finance such programs. As has been noted, some teachers were refusing to return to the school, while others were deciding to leave the profession altogether. School climate was problematic.

CHARACTERISTICS THAT FOSTER
A POSITIVE CLIMATE

There are six characteristics that foster a positive climate, as follows. They continue the attention given to organizational climate and its important impact on policy and regulation development.

1. FOCUS

A set of shared goals, clear-cut, but with expanding dimensions. Such goals are set forth in the organization's policies. The term *clear-cut* infers that the stated goals represent the purposes and the organized way of implementing them represents the organization's regulations. A positive climate requires some organized way of examining its goals. In addition, the organization continues to operate with its original and different objectives.

2. SELF-IMAGE AND UNIQUE PERCEPTION

Personnel in the organization are aware of the system's purposes even though they might not fully agree with them. In any case, personnel give the best that they have to offer until the policy/regulation at hand demonstrates its importance to the purposes in place.

3. PERSONAL GROWTH IS PRIZED

Opportunities for self-improvement are provided. Research has demonstrated the fact that personnel tend to leave the organization if opportunities for self-development/growth are not available.

4. REWARDS FOR ACHIEVEMENT

Rewards and recognition are given on the basis of merit. Although organizational goals are viewed as a system consideration, individualized goals that have been determined by the employee and supervisor are viewed as being of paramount importance.

5. NEW IDEAS AND WORKLIFE IMPROVEMENTS

New ideas by personnel are evaluated on the basis of their merit versus the source of their origin. Idea people are purposely recruited. Various strategies are implemented to gain new ideas such as shadow groups, task force groups serve as think tanks, open channels of communication are established, pilot programs are initiated, and praise is given in positive ways for "creative thinking" that leads to improved procedures.

6. FLUIDITY OF INTERNAL STRUCTURE

The organization sets forth ways to combat becoming a prisoner of its own procedures. The organization is interested in what it should become rather than what it has done. It develops a discontent with the status quo. It sets forth procedures to assess and evaluate its manual of policies and regulations.

School Climates Determinants—Phi Delta Kappa Publication

Phi Delta Kappa set forth the characteristics of climate determinants in the CKF Ltd. work, as follows. School climate determinants were identified in the three specific categories of program determinants, process determinants, and material determinants. As noted by Phi Delta Kappa, program activities and requirements are designed so as they are consistent with the everchanging intellectual, social, and physical developmental characteristics of pupils as they grow.

School Climate Determinants

Program Determinants	Process Determinants	Material Determinants
Opportunities for Active Learning	Problem-Solving Ability	Adequate Resources
Individual Performance Expectations	Improvement of Goals	Supportive and Efficient
Logistic System		
Varied Learning Environments	Working with Conflicts	Suitability of Plan
Flexibility of Curriculum	Effective Communications	

Support Structure—
    Appropriate
Policies Cooperatively
    Determined
Varied Reward System

Autonomy and
    Accountability
Ability to Plan for the
    Future

A Summary School Climate Assessment Profile Form
Name of School:_____

Section A—General Climate Factors Revealed in School Environment, Personnel, and Practice

RUBRIC

Climate Factors Revealed	Almost Never	Occasionally	Frequently	Almost Always
	0	1	2	3
A. General Climate Factors				
1. Respect	____	____	____	____
2. Trust	____	____	____	____
3. High Morale	____	____	____	____
4. Involvement/Input	____	____	____	____
5. Growth Opportunities	____	____	____	____
6. Cooperative Activities	____	____	____	____
7. Positive Relationships	____	____	____	____
8. Caring Atmosphere	____	____	____	____
B. Program Determinants				
1. Active Learning Environment	____	____	____	____
2. Varied Curriculum/Needs	____	____	____	____
3. Varied Reward System	____	____	____	____
4. Cooperative Learning Sessions	____	____	____	____
5. Extracurricular Activities	____	____	____	____

C. Process Determinants
   1. Problem Solving
      Strategies   ____   ____   ____   ____
   2. Assessment of
      School Goals   ____   ____   ____   ____
   3. Working
      with Conflicts
   4. Effective
      Communications
   5. Effective Learning
      Strategies
   6. Decision Making
      Involvement
   7. Assessment/
      Evaluation of Goals

D. Material Determinants
   1. Adequate Resources
   2. Supportive
      Logistic System
   3. Adequacy of
      School Plant

Summary: Of course, the entries in each of the four major determinant categories can be changed in order to meet the requirements of the school being assessed. Some schools might want to use a rubric of some kind to reach a final scoring note of poor, fair, good, very good, and excellent (e.g., 0–23, poor to fair; 24–45, fair to good; and 46–69, good to very good). The final score might be helpful, but it is not an absolute. Like any other assessment form, the climate rating score simply gives you some idea as to the climate rating of the school and can be compared to previous or future climate assessment ratings.

An Example of One Section of a School District's Personnel Policy System

The following example of one section (Personnel) of a school district's policy manual demonstrates the major sections, subsections, divisions, subdivisions, items, and subitems of the manual's content. Keep in mind that the entries are topical only, and the content of each entry is added as fits the case in each separate school district. Once again, it is important for the reader to note that the numbers for each entry (e.g., 4118.231) represent the fourth series, first subseries, first division, eighth subdivision, second item, third subitem, and first "digit" in the personnel listing. Check closely for the codification strategy set forth in the table that follows.

Table 3.1. Section 4000, Personnel, of the Davies-Brickell Policy System

Article	Personnel	Series
0. Concept and Roles in Personnel		4000
A. Goals and Objectives		4010
1. Certificated Personnel		4100
A. Permanent Personnel		4110
1. Recruitment and Selection		4111
a. Equal Employment Opportunity		4111.1
b. Vacancies		4111.2
2. Appointment and Conditions of Employment		4112
a. Contract		4112.1
b. Certification		4112.2
c. Oaths		4112.3
d. Health Information		4112.4
e. Security		4112.5
f. Personnel Records		4112.6
g. Orientation		4112.7
h. Nepotism		4112.8
i. Staff Health & Safety		4112.9
(1) Communication Diseases		4112.91
a. HIV-AIDS		4112.911
3. Assignment & Transfers		4113
a. Load/Scheduling/Hours of Employment		4113.1
b. Promotions/Demotions		4113.2
c. Work Year		4113.3
d. Job Sharing		4113.4
4.Transfer/Reassignment		4114
5. Evaluation/Supervision		4115
6. Probation/Tenure Status		4116
a. Seniority		4116.1
7. Separation/Disciplinary Action		4117
a. Retirement		4117.1
b. Resignation		4117.2
c. Personnel Reduction		4117.3
d. Dismissal/Suspension		4117.4
(1) Just Cause		4117.41
(2) Notice; Hearing		4117.42
(3) Right of Appeal		4117.43

Article	Personnel	Series
8. Rights, Responsibilities, and Duties		4118
a. Civil and Legal Rights		4118.1
(1) Nondiscrimination		4118.11
(a) Grievance Procedure, Title IX		4118.111
(2) Freedom of Speech		4118.12
(3) Conflict of Interest		4118.13
(4)		4118.14
b. Professional Responsibilities		4118.2
(1) Academic Freedom		4118.21
(2) Code of Ethics		4118.22
(3) Conduct of Dress		4113.23
(a) Smoking, Drinking, Use of Drugs on School Premises		4118.231
(4) Staff/Student Relations		4118.24
c. Duties		4118.3

Summary: There are several additional sections in the foregoing personnel policy, including: Temporary and Part-Time Personnel, Activities, Compensation and Related Benefits, Leaves and Vacations, Noncertificated Personnel, Position Assignments, and others. Chapter 4 will place an emphasis on policy and regulation manuals for a variety of programs, companies, and organizations.

TRUE OR FALSE QUIZ

1. The most important responsibility of a local school board is to develop the administrative regulations for implementing the school district's policies. True____ or False____
2. If a school district appears to be doing well, it has little need for wasting time to develop a policy manual. True____ or False____
3. An effective school policy serves to answer the question of how to implement effective administrative regulations. True____ or False____
4. Compliance refers to the duty of the organization to obey the laws relating to governance. True____ or False____
5. According to the National Association of School Psychology, policies tend to interfere with a school board's autonomy for directing a school district. True____ or False____
6. Since policies are established to resolve problems, strong language best suits the way in which they should be worded. True____ or False____
7. Unfortunately, school rules for students have been found to hinder rather than help student behavior in schools. True ____or False____

8. A policy manual is seldom needed in organizations that have a positive climate. True _____ or False_____
9. Unfortunately, rules for students in schools have been found to hinder rather than improve student behavior. True_____ or False___
10. School climate and school culture are viewed as being synonymous when used in education. True___ or False_____
11. Although climate has been found to enhance good relationships, it has yet to be found as a positive learning characteristic. True__ or False_____
12. Knowing the community generally refers to being well acquainted with its history, climate, and culture. True_____ or False_____
13. Unfortunately, a strategy for determining the climate of a school or organization has yet to be developed. True_____ or False_____
14. Organizational climate, just like organizational culture, is a constant that seldom, if ever, changes. True_____ or False_____
15. In a study by the Department of Troublesome Research (DTR), it was found that an effective set of organizational policies and regulations has no effect on the learning culture of a school. True_____ or False_____

Answers to the Quiz: Only Questions 4 and 12 are **True**. All other statements are **False**.

Comments on Quiz Entries

1. (Statement #1 is false.) The local school board is legally responsibility for both the policies and regulations of the school district. However, common practice is for the board to develop school policies and delegate the development of the administrative regulations to the superintendent and staff. From a legal standpoint, however, the development of both policies and regulations has been delegated to the local school board by the state Department of Education. That is, the U.S. Constitution has delegated all education responsibilities, not mentioned in the Constitution, to the various states. In turn, and most commonly, the states have delegated local education governance states. In turn, the states have delegated local policy development to the local school boards.
2. (Statement #2 is false.) If an organization is doing well, it is highly likely that it has developed and implemented an effective policy manual. As underscored in this chapter, school systems with effective policy manuals also have healthy climates and a positive learning culture. It is not to say that schools with effective policy manuals do not face difficult times, because various problems are apparent in most every

active organization. Policy manuals, however, provide ways to meet and resolve difficult problems. When policy manual development includes direct involvement of organization personnel, such practices enhance the chances that the problem at hand will be better understood and more readily resolved.

3. (Statement #3 is false.) It must be understood that question #3 is speaking of policy rather than the policy manual. Chapter 1 noted that policies differ from administrative regulations. A policy answers the question of "what is to be done" and not "how something is to be done." However, it is not unusual for a regulation to accompany a policy statement. If the school board wants to emphasize how it wants a stated policy to be implemented, it is not unusual for it to include regulatory directions within the policy statement.

4. (Statement #4 is true.) Compliance requirements include the local, state, and federal laws, statutes, and regulations that school boards (and organizations) must obey in their stated policies and regulations. In fact, when the state or federal government passes a law that centers on organizational governance, it is viewed as a "policy" requirement for school boards and other organizations as well. Federal and state control has been an ongoing controversy in America. Federal program policies related to education have been ongoing for several decades. However, if the local school district wants the funds related to various programs that the federal government wants to implement, the money only follows when the federal program is actually implemented at the local level.

5. (Statement #5 is false.) Of course, the oppositive is the positive result. Effective policy and regulation development promote the authority and control of school programming by the local school board. In fact, policy and administrative regulation development is viewed as the school board's primary responsibility. Some people would argue that hiring the school superintendent is a school board's most important responsibility. Although the hiring of a superintendent is a high order, we give policy and regulation development first place. Unfortunately, all too many school boards purchase their policy manuals from their state education offices. This unfortunate practice is, in our opinion, why education in America is not rated #1 in the world, but commonly is rated as low as #15 in many assessment polls.

6. (Statement #6 is false.) Positive language rather than strong language is best suited for policy statements. Strong language tends to be offensive rather than being helpful for directing the desired behaviors. Positive language serves to promote positive results.

7. (Statement #7 is false.) School rules for students have been found to be positive provisions for students. Rules help students know what positive

behaviors are expected and thus give them a standard for their behavior. When students have some involvement in developing the rules, the climate of the school becomes more positive.

8. (Statement #8 is false.) On the contrary, positive climates in schools commonly are conditioned by the fact that a viable set of rules have been cooperatively developed and implemented in the school.

9. (Statement #9 is false.) As noted in the answers to questions #7 and #8, school rules serve to enhance student behavior. Proper behavior is set forth for students to know and understand. With an understanding of what behavior is expected, the climate of student relationships is more likely to be positive. If students have had some involvement in establishing the behavioral standards, many problems will be resolved by the student body itself.

10. (Statement #10 is false.) Although climate and culture have some common links, they do have significant differences. Culture is the set of important beliefs and values that members of the organization share. It is more normative than climate in the sense that it is a reflection of the shared values, beliefs, and underlying assumptions of its members across an array of organizational dimensions that include but go beyond interpersonal relationships. Climate is the collective personality of a school or organization. It is the atmosphere that prevails as characterized by the social and professional interactions of people.

11. (Statement #11 is false.) Several research studies and assessments have demonstrated that positive climates in school settings serve positively toward the school's learning process.

12. (Statement #12 is true.) Knowing the community centers on the importance of being knowledgeable of its culture. What is important regarding the goals and objectives of the community's people? What education objectives are of major importance? What leadership activities are of major importance for achieving the needs of community members? What is the power structure that is operating in the community? How can positive communication among the organization and community members be fostered? How are important program needs accomplished? The foregoing questions are examples of ways and means for knowing the community in which one operates.

13. (Statement #13 is false.) On the contrary, several different strategies have been developed for assessing an organization's climate. For education, the Organizational Climate Description Questionnaire (OCDQ) has served hundreds of schools in the United States. This assessment instrument serves to describe school climates from being open to

closed. An open climate is described as having high staff morale, effective communication systems, positive socialization, and attainment of positive goals.

14. (Statement #14 is false.) Organizational climate in organizations, just like the weather, tends to change. However, many organizational climates change from closed to open or from poor to good. No organization has a magic wand to change its climate. However, practice has shown that those organizations that work on policy and regulation as on ongoing process tend to have positive, open organizational results.

15. (Statement #15 is false.) Organizations, including schools, that have an ongoing process for policy and regulation development, have been shown to be more effective than those that do not have such a process. Policies that serve to keep the organization's purposes in place and its regulations in order enhance the probability of its future success.

KEY CHAPTER IDEAS AND RECOMMENDATIONS

- Policy and regulation development and implementation are the primary responsibilities of the local school board. However, the development and implementation of administrative regulations commonly is delegated to the local school superintendent and staff.
- School purposes and conditions do differ. Thus, local school board processes should be in place for implementing policy development as an ongoing process.
- School board membership requirements in almost every state are minimal. Membership qualifications for school board members should be studied and set forth as a legal requirement.
- The language of organizational policies and regulations is of paramount importance. Positive language is highly recommended.
- Legal compliance by organizations is absolute. Local school policies and regulations should be examined by legal counselors to obviate potential problems.
- Contrary to beliefs on the part of some people, positive school discipline rules have been found to strengthen good behavior on the part of students.
- The climate of a school or another organization indeed can be assessed and evaluated. The Organizational Climate Description Questionnaire by Halpin and Croft has been used by many schools to determine their climate status.

- The common statement of "Know Your Community" has been implemented in hundreds of cases and utilized for making policy and regulation processes a positive success.

REFERENCES

Bentley, R. R., and A. M. Rempel. (1970). *Purdue Teacher Opinionnaire.* West Lafayette, IN: Purdue Research Foundation.

Halpin, A., and D. B. Croft. (1962). *The Organization Climate of Schools.* U.S. Office of Education Research Project (Contract #SAE 543-8639). Chicago: Midwest Administration Center.

Kunichoff, Y. (2022). "Security Risks at School." *Arizona Republic*, vol. 133, no. 20, 1A.

McMenemy, L. (2021). *Policies and Legislation.* https://ogletree.com/.

National Association of School Psychologists (NASP). (2018). *Effective School Discipline.* https://www.nasponline.org/discipline.

Norton, M. S. (2008). *Human Resources Administration for Educational Leaders.* Thousand Oaks, CA: Sage.

Norton, M. S. (1968). "Know Your Community in Ten Easy Lessons." *Clearing House*, vol. 43, no. 1. Taylor & Francis, Ltd.

Pai, Y., and S. Adler. (2001). *Cultural Foundations of Education* (4th Ed.). Merrill Publications.

Schein, E. (2010). *Organizational Culture and Leadership.* San Francisco, CA: Jossey-Bass.

Stern, G. G. (1964). *High School Characteristics Index.* Syracuse, NY: Psychological Research Center, Syracuse University.

Chapter 4

Examples of Policy Manuals

The primary goal of this chapter is to present and discuss policy and regulation manual examples from the wide worlds of education, business, and industry.

This chapter centers on the examination of policy and regulation documents from a wide variety of organizations. Previous policy examples presented in chapters 1, 2, and 3 most often had some system of codifying each manual topic using a numeric or alpha system. The majority of manual examples considered in this chapter do not use such coding systems, although many manuals do use some method of identifying a policy by using some form of numbering or bullets to note separate entries.

One interesting policy manual example focuses on insurance (Insurance Center Group). Major sections of the policy manual include Quoting, Writing Business, Service, Claims, General Guidelines, Office Practices, Marketing, Commissions, and a last section on the Bank Policy Manual Definition. These eight sections constitute some 75 pages of the manual.

We found the Bank Policy Manual Definition section to be of special interest. That statement follows:

THE BANK POLICY MANUAL DEFINITION

The *Bank Policy Manual* is the governing body of documentation that defines and clarifies a bank's policies and procedures. These manuals are generally divided into sections that identify a specific element within an organization (Administration, Compliance, Lending, Operational, etc.) and may be assigned a number series for identity purposes. Within these sections are numerous supporting policies and procedures.

Need some helpful pointers in developing your policy and procedures? BankPolicies.com is the most trusted resource for bank policies online, and we offer a vast array of bank policy templates that are easy to customize to sluit the specific needs of your bank, credit union, fintech company, or other type of financial institution and help you stay on top of regulatory changes such as those issued by the Consumer Finance Protection Bureau (CFPB), Federal Deposit Insurance Company (FDIC), Federal Reserve, Office of the Comptroller of the Currency (OCC), or other federal regulatory bodies and industry recommended best practices.

In addition, we recommend you visit our Bank Policy Writing Tips page to gain some insightful information and recommended industry best practices. Policies and procedures are the heart of any Policy Manual, and it is important to understand the differences between a "policy" and a "procedure."

DEFINITIONS OF THE TERMS *POLICY* AND *REGULATIONS* (PROCEDURES) FROM A BANKER'S VIEWPOINT

From a banker's viewpoint, policies and procedures are the heart of any policy manual, and it is important to understand the difference between a policy and a procedure.

The *Bank Policy Manual* (BankPolicies.com, 2022) defined a policy as a high-level overall plan that embraces the general goals and directives of a bank. Procedures are documented steps or activities that serve to accomplish the goals of a related policy. Bank information mentions other important considerations, such as revisions. It is not unusual for a properly written manual to remain without revision for extended periods of time. There are, however, times when improvements, changes, or alterations are necessary. Experience has shown that procedures, more than policies, require assessment and evaluation. Procedures are implemented on a daily basis, and organizational change is ongoing.

Those personnel who implement procedures on a daily basis are in the best position to recommend new procedures that serve to meet the goals of the organization. Nevertheless, the bank's governance board must receive the request for changes in procedures before they are implemented. This requirement is virtually the same as the procedure that is implemented by a school board within a school district.

POLICY AND REGULATION MANUALS
FOR RETAIL STORES

Waters (2019) sets forth policies and rules for retail stores. Primary attention is given to types of payment, product pricing, layaway, special orders, hours of operation, returns and exchanges, and other store activities such as housekeeping, gift wrapping, theft, shoplifting, delivery service, power failure procedures, and other customer services. Waters sets forth the following policy recommendations:

- The best time to establish policies and procedures for a retail store is during the planning stages.
- Each policy and procedure should be set forth in a policy/procedure handbook.
- Each store employee should have the policy manual at hand. The manual should include how store employees should handle various items of business: What forms to accept, how to handle payments by check, and does the store offer employee, military, or other purchasing discounts?
- How does the store handle returns and exchanges?
- What holidays will the store close?
- What are the store's shoplifting policy and procedures?
- What procedures are in place for handling of a power failure?

Waters recommends that store policies and procedures should serve as a guide rather than being absolute and unreasonable. Store policies and regulations should be posted for customers to see.

One idea would be to list some policies and procedures on the purchase receipts. Times and business procedures do change. The assessment and evaluation of the store's policies and procedures must be assessed and evaluated periodically.

WHAT IS PUBLIC POLICY?

A Live Career staff writer (2022) authored an article that focused on answering the question: "What is public policy?" The article opens by stating, "A Government is a body of people that work to effectively and successfully guide a unit or community. One thing government does is set and administer policy." That is, government policies contain the reasons things are done in a certain way and why. There are four types of public policies: regulatory, constituent, distributive, and redistributive.

Regulatory public policy is in play when a government defines the boundaries of what actions will be allowed and what actions will not be allowed.

The economic and social welfare of both people and organizations are controlled as to what they can do. Policies on topics such as abortion, gun control, marijuana, and alcohol purchases commonly are topics within the regulatory policy controls.

Constituent public policy is related to the way government is structured. Such actions as the establishment of the Department of Homeland Security (DHS) 20 years ago. Other acts, such as The Administrative Procedure Act of 1946, The Works Progress Administration Act of 1935, and the way states handle electoral votes are examples of constituent public policy actions. Disasters that are assisted by the Federal Emergency Management Agency (FEMA) are examples of constituent public policy. In recent times, such disasters as tornadoes, floods, wildfires, and gun shootings have called upon FEMA for assistance. Constituent policy comes into play in each of these disasters.

Distributive public policy focuses on the use of money to fund public services (e.g., free lunch in schools, COVID-19 vaccines, school bus transportation, school building projects, school vouchers, maintenance of roads and bridges). Distributive funding might benefit only a small group of individuals or large groups of individuals such as the free lunch programs provided in some schools. The bottom line, however, is vested in the way distributive funding serves in a positive way to impact on doing good for individuals or for organization that are doing positive things for communities.

Redistributive public policy centers on the redistribution of funds to benefit a particular group of people. One contemporary example of this policy is The American Rescue Act of 2021 (LiveCareer, 2022). This act focused on providing relief to individuals who experienced economic losses tied to the COVID-19 pandemic. The redistributive policy rationale was in practice. Acts such as the Temporary Assistance for Needy Families and Department of Education Act that distributed funds to college students are examples of redistributed public policy.

Food Safety & Quality Control Manual

The *Food Safety & Quality Control Manual* (American Friends Service Committee, 2016) is of special interest. The manual, as developed by the American Friends Service Committee, contains seven major sections and nine information sections in the appendices.

The manual's table of contents is set forth as follows:

TABLE OF CONTENTS

Section 1: Traceability Program

Farm Map, Harvest Log, Product Recall

Section 2: Harvesting

Employee Health and Hygiene, Harvest Containers and Tools,
Sanitizing Harvesting Equipment

Section 3: Washing

Sanitizing of Washing Surfaces

Sanitizing of Salad Spinner and Tools

Wash Procedures

Section 4: Packing

Invoicing Procedures

Section 5: Storing

Section 6: Transporting

Section 7: Resources

Appendix

Appendix A: Example Farm Map(s)

Appendix B: Example Harvest Log

Appendix C: Example of Buyer Contact Information

Appendix D: Example Product Recall Log

Appendix E: Example Employee Health and Hygiene Policy

Appendix F: Example General Harvest Cleaning Log

Appendix G: Example Food Safety Checklist

Appendix H: Example Product Specifications

Appendix I: Example Product Storage Temperature Chart

Perhaps you found the foregoing policy example interesting. However, we point out that the sample herein did not include related policy content actually used in the *Food Safety & Quality Control Manual*. For example, Appendix

H, Example Product Specifications, sets forth policy specifications for handling one product, that of spinach. The standard for handling is as follows: Quality, Harvest Tips, Handling and Packing, Washing, Packing, and details relating to Sanitizing and Packaging.

Keep in mind that the purpose here is related to the *policy standards* set forth by the Agricultural Financial Services Corporation) (AFSC) for food handling. Just how the food handling process is conducted is not the primary focus. Rather, the comprehensiveness of the policies/regulations for processing the foods is of primary interest. The policies for food handling are not only established but are set forth in specific detail. As stated by the company, food safety is a growing concern. A food safety program is being required in an increasing number of farmers and company workers. The company's policies are meant to support farmers in food safety and consistency in quality control.

POLICIES AND PROCEDURES FOR CAR DEALERS

The following policies and procedures are set forth by Gerton Auto Sales, Inc. (2022). The warranty policies are set forth in specific terms that do appear to be rather negative and self-serving, but do state that they are governed by the laws of the State of Indiana.

POLICIES & PROCEDURES

Warranty Information and Terms and Conditions
As-Is-No Warranty

To the best of our knowledge the manufacturer's warranty has expired on pre-owned vehicles. Consult the manufacturer's warranty booklet for details as to warranty coverage, service location, etc., for new vehicles as well as pre-owned vehicles where the balance of the Manufacturer's warranty has not yet expired. Gerton Auto Sales, Inc. sells all vehicles AS-IS WHERE-IS and assumes no responsibility for any repairs. All warranty coverage, if any, comes from the unexpected manufacturer's warranty.

The seller shall not be responsible for the correct description, authenticity, genuineness, or defects herein, and makes no warranty in connection therewith. No allowance or set aside will be made on account of any incorrectness, imperfection, defect, or damage.

This policy goes on to say what other provisions the company will not do and so forth. Legality, deposits, fees, sales tax, and other buyer responsibilities are stated in the policy statement, including pickup and shipping responsibilities of the buyer. Although this entry is quite different from other company policy and regulation statements from the business world, it is included due to the fact that it is much different than business policies and procedures of other businesses.

Motor Vehicle Dealer—2018 Edition

A motor vehicle manual was published by the Enforcement Division of the Texas Department of Motor Vehicles in 2018. The director of the division states that the purpose of the policy manual is to provide prospective and current motor vehicle industry licensees as well as other stakeholders with an easy-to-use overview of Texas motor vehicle dealer licensing and operating laws. He states that, "Our goal is that licensees comply with the laws regulating the industry" (p. i).

The manual contains six major chapters: Chapter 1. Definitions Used in This Manual; Chapter 2. Enforcement and Motor Vehicle Divisions; Chapter 3. Licensing; Chapter 4. Compliance & Dealer Operations; Chapter 5. Cash Sales, Seller Financing, Retail Installment Contracts and Repossessions; and Chapter 6. Titling Vehicles. Each entry under the six sections is coded and named. For example, in the index for Chapter 2, there are only three entries: History (2.1), The Enforcement Division (2.2), and The Motor Vehicle Division (2.3). Chapter 4 has four sections that include Codes and Rules, Record Keeping Requirements, Consignment Sales, and Blue Law.

Chapter 6 of the manual has 44 subsections that include topics such as Forging Title Documents Is a Felony, Used Car Buyer's Sales, Odometer Rollbacks, and Lost Titles. These entries in the motor vehicle manual would be considered as the "administrative" regulations. The comprehensiveness and detail of the motor vehicle dealer's manual are impressive. It is somewhat comforting to know that licensed car dealers are governed by official policies and regulations. Legal compliance plays a large role in the car dealer's worklife.

HEALTHCARE POLICY EXAMPLES

Healthcare is a difficult area for completing a single policy manual that "governs" the expanding purposes and procedures that accompany the topic. However, it is possible to underscore the importance of policies and procedures in this area and the important procedures for developing manuals in this area.

As noted by NEOGOV (2020), healthcare policies improve operational excellence and patient care. Policies and procedures are an incredibly important part of making sure the staff knows how to care for patients and do their job effectively.

Healthcare Compliance Manual, Chapter 3 Contents

Chapter 3 Running an Effective Compliance Program
    Introduction to Running an Effective Compliance Program
    Developing Core Departmental Relationships
    Conducting an Organizational Compliance Assessment
    Hiring Compliance Staff
    Building Trust with Senior Management and the Board
    Educating the Board and Defining Its Role
        Risk Assessment and Management
    Compliance Policies, Procedures, and Codes of Conduct
Compliance Training
Internal Reporting Systems

The resources associated with each of the major topics in Chapter 3 also are included in the policy manual's chapter listings. For example, for the Internal Reporting Systems topic, Non-Retaliation Policy samples serve as resources.

SPEAKING OF RETAIL POLICIES

Other policy examples will be presented later in the chapter, but it looms important to keep in mind just how and why effective policies can help an organization succeed. Funk (2017) set forth five essential retail policies that can help an organization succeed. Funk focused on retail policies. She recommends that policies should be established before one's retail business opens the door. Policies that you put in place are what will ultimately drive the success of your business.

One important policy that must be put into place centers on the way financial operations are handled. The polices on *payment handling* are of paramount importance. One leading question to be answered is your handling of money. For example, will you accept checks? If so, on what basis? A straightforward written policy could set forth the guidelines for answering that question.

A second question set forth by Funk is "What will be your hours for store operation?" That's a simple question, or is it? The hours of store operation, holidays, weekends, preparing the store for opening, store closeup for restocking store shelves, cleanup, and reordering must be kept in mind. What special store services will be performed? Will your store have delivery service? What personnel must be hired?

Customer service looms important in most every retail store. What about return items? How will this frequent happening be handled? Is shoplifting a potential problem in your situation, and if so, what security measures will be implemented?

Custodial services are vitally important in most every retail store. When will cleanups be accomplished during store hours, if any? How are store monies to be handled? How much money will be kept within the store during store hours? What security measures must be attended during the store's closing hours? In many retail stores, is security during closing hours of major importance?

The final question is this: Have you developed policies and regulations for dealing with the many matters suggested in the foregoing discussion? The store will change over the years. What are your processes for assessing, evaluating, and updating the store's policy manual in an ongoing and ever-changing environment?

SAMPLE POLICIES AND PROCEDURES
MANUAL FOR NONPROFITS

The following policies and procedures manual was developed to assist Non-Federal Entities (NFEs) in their administration of federal funds. This manual's table of contents alone assumes over four pages. The manual has two specific purposes: (1) to provide emerging NFEs with sample policies and procedures so that they would be able to develop them for their own specific purposes and (2) to provide the same policies and procedures to compare with their existing manual and assess and evaluate the ones in place.

The major sections of the NFE manual are listed as follows. The contents of one section are listed to demonstrate the comprehensiveness of the manual.

THE NFE POLICIES AND PROCEDURES MANUAL

Table of Contents

Personnel Policies

Performance and Discipline

THE NFE POLICY FOR PERFORMANCE AND DISCIPLINE

Pay Raises and Bonuses

Pay raises and bonuses (if applicable) will be determined annually by the Board of Directors and the Office in question. In the event that there are monies available for compensation increases, these increases will be paid as salary and/or bonus according to exempt or non-exempt status and determined by attainment of performance standards.

Bonus compensation may only be paid to exempt staff. Bonuses are based on goal achievement in the previous year and are paid to both reward over achievement and as an incentive to continue future performance. Like pay raises, bonus pay will be paid as salary.

Performance Appraisals

The Performance Appraisal Process for Exempt and Non-Exempt employees is the foundation for all compensation activity and provides a unique opportunity to unite the employee's accountabilities and achievements to the objectives and strategic plans of the organization.

Supervision and Evaluation

The Chairman of the Board of Directors is the direct supervisor of the organization in question and in conjunction with the Executive Committee of the Board of Directors will conduct and annual performance evaluation of the Executive Director. The Executive Director is the direct supervisor of each individual employee. In the case that there are Program Directors, the Program Directors are the direct supervisors of the support staff in their program.

Performance Evaluations

The organization in question believes in the importance of employee performance evaluations. All employees will be evaluated by their direct supervisor using established standards of performance for their position, on a semi-annual basis in January and June. The evaluation is based in job performance with regard to applicable skills, productivity, quality of work, attitude and cooperation, dependability, job knowledge, effectiveness, and other areas applicable to specific employee categories. Attendance and punctuality are a major factor in an employee's overall review.

Initial Evaluation

The immediate supervisor or the Executive Director will perform an evaluation three months after the employment with the organization.

Corrective Action and Employment Termination

Most employees want to do a good job. Supervisors shall help employees succeed on the job by:

a. Providing a thorough orientation for new employees
b. Clearly establishing expectations for behavior and performance
c. Providing training, coaching, and mentoring
d. Providing feedback through appropriate supervision

However, in every workplace there will be situations where an employee fails to meet expectations or where an employee commits acts of misconduct. There may be times when, despite all of the supervisor's best efforts, the employee continues to demonstrate unsatisfactory performance or problem behavior.

Forms of Corrective Action

When corrective action is necessary, the amount and type of action taken depends on the particular circumstances. The organization maintains the discretion to determine what corrective action is appropriate in each situation, regardless of what correction the employee may have received previously. For example, in some circumstances, it may be appropriate to give an additional written warning before taken any stronger action, while in other circumstances it may be appropriate to take strong actions, including termination, without any previous warnings or suspensions.

Though other forms of corrective action are also possible, these are the types most often taken.

a. **Counseling:** If a supervisor becomes concerned about an employee's performance at work, she or he may meet with the employee to discuss certain concerns and develop ways to address the concerns.

b. **Oral Warning:** The supervisor meets with the employee to review the prior discussions and state his/her continuing concerns with the employee's performance. The supervisor should clearly identify the purpose of this meeting as an oral warning, which is part of the corrective action. A summary of the oral warning meeting may be given to the employee with a copy retained by the supervisor and a copy kept in the employee's personnel file.

c. **Written Warning:** If the employee's performance does not improve after an oral warning, or if circumstances otherwise warrant, it may be necessary to give a written warning to an employee which may include the following:

    i. Current level of performance and areas requiring improvement

ii. Specific level of performance expected in each of the identified deficiencies
iii. Time frame for improvement
iv. Steps the supervisor will take to support improvement
v. Specified time for follow-up meeting
vi. Consequences if performance does not improve

The employee should read and sign the written warning. In signing, the employee acknowledges that he or she has read and understood the document. The signature does not imply agreement.

d. **Termination:** The organization may dismiss an employee when this action is in the organization's best interests. Employees should remember that employment is to be carried by the mutual consent clause. Both the employee and the agency are free to terminate the employment relationship at any time and for any reason.

Occasions for Corrective Action

Listed below are some of the kinds of behavior or performance that may lead to corrective action. It is, of course, not possible to list all of the kinds of problems that may occur in the work place; other kinds of behavior or performance may also lead to corrective action.

a. Unsatisfactory job performance
b. Excessive absenteeism or tardiness, or failure to contact supervisor about absence
c. Violation of the organization's procedures or rules
d. Theft or willful damage of the property of the agency or other employees
e. Refusal to perform work as directed or willful neglect of duties
f. Violent or abusive behavior or language
g. Acceptance of any gifts, favors, other remuneration from any individual or firm having or proposing to have any relationship with the organization

WAYNE STATE UNIVERSITY POLICIES

The Wayne State University Secretary/Office of the President and the Division of Finance and Business/Office of the Vice President, coordinates the editing, review, issuance, and archiving of all official Wayne State University policies.

Policy subjects within this site are presented in 12 sections: Academic, Administrative (general), Budget, Computing and Information Technology, Equal Opportunity, Finance and Business Operations (i.e., Business & Auxiliary Operations, Facilities Planning & Management, Fiscal Operations, Human Resources, Procurement & Strategic Sourcing and Risk Management), Labor Relations, Legal, Public Safety, Research, Student, and Other.

Within each section, you will find standardized policies that have been created through the WSU official development and approval process and other resources to aid university personnel in conducting and managing the day-to-day university business affairs.

WSU policies clarify the institution's expectations of its faculty, staff, and students, mitigate institutional risks, improve efficiency and effectiveness, as well as support the university's best practices.

The documentation of university policies and procedures promotes the standardization and simplification of administrative functions and is a reference for those who have administrative responsibilities within the university.

Please refer to the WSU Policy Levels and Manuals option from the left menu of this page for additional information

NEWS

August 2020 University Policy Updates

WSU Policy Statement Examples

AN EXAMPLE OF AN EDUCATIONAL POLICY
THAT INCLUDES REGULATORY CRITERIA

The following policy example centers on the human resources program and the specific recruitment and selection of personnel. Keep in mind that the terms *section* and *series* are used interchangeably.

SECTION 4000 PERSONNEL

It is the responsibility of the superintendent of schools and persons delegated by him or her to determine the personnel needs of the school district and to locate qualified candidates to recommend for employment to the school board.

There shall be no discrimination in any applicant by reason of race, color, national origin, creed, marital status, sex, or age.

It shall be the duty of the school superintendent to see that persons nominated for employment meet all the qualifications established by law and the school board for the type of position for which the hiring nomination is made. Professional staff, clerical staff, custodial staff, health staff, and all other service positions in the school district are included in the recruitment and selection requirements set forth.

Legal Reference: A.S.A

15.3119 Superintendent and other personnel; qualifications; powers and duties

15.3569 hiring of teachers; contracts. Lafayette School District, South Lafayette

Date of Policy Acceptance:_____

PERSONNEL

A Numeric Sample of a School Board Policy on Personnel

ARTICLE 4   (Series 4000)

Whenever the number 4 leads the entry, it is related to personnel (4000). As previously noted, other numbers are used to indicate the subsection, division, subdivision, item, and subitem. For example, the code number 4121.13 refers to section 4, subsection 1, division 2, subdivision 1, item 1, and subitem 3.

As noted in the foregoing Davies-Brickell model, only nine major series can be considered for inclusion in the policy manual. If the school district wanted to add two other major series to their policies, the numbers 10,000 and 11,000 would have to be utilized. However, such an addition is not possible. If the number 10 were to be inserted in any code number, it would skew the reading incorrectly. Thus, the Alpha System is favored in many cases since the alphabet includes 26 letters from A to Z. Since the National School Boards Association uses the Alpha Coding System, most school districts in America have that system.

It is common knowledge that most institutions of higher learning have special units for presidential leadership, student services, health services, college programs, departments, athletics, and other divisional units. It is common for each of these programs to have a policy and regulation manual. The Emeritus College at Arizona State University does not have a policy and regulation manual as such, although the college does have a historical statement that includes certain purposes and program activities.

A policy manual for the ASU Emeritus College was proposed in 2019 but has not been officially adopted by the college or by Arizona State University to date. Nevertheless, for the purposes of this book, a sample of the proposed policy manual is noted herein.

The codification method for the Emeritus College policy manual is the numerical system. The primary series for the manual are Foundations and Basic Commitments (1000); Business Operations & Fiscal Management (2000); Governance, Administration, and Operations (3000); University and Community Relationships (4000); Program Activities and Member University Involvement (5000); Meetings of the Emeritus College (6000); Program Reports and Communication Activities (7000); and Emeritus College Committees (8000).

We submit that a policy and regulation manual would serve to improve every department and college within an institution of higher learning. Faculty and staff personnel, as well as students, constantly are changing in colleges and universities throughout the nation. Orientation efforts for all personnel could be improved if some special attention to the organization's policies and regulations was given to its purposes and requirements.

A proposed policy manual for the Emeritus College of one university sets forth the purposes in its opening preamble:

> The Emeritus College of this university was founded seventeen years ago for the purpose of giving a home to intellectual, creative, and college engagement of retired emeritus faculty with the University. As an academic unit within the university, the College serves its members, the University, and the community as a center for the resources made available by both the membership and the University. The College provides an organization base for official University ties, emeritus policy, and programmatic development. As previously noted, eight primary series are included the policy manual: Foundations and Basic Commitments (1000); Business Operations & Fiscal Management (2000); Governance, Administration, and Operations (3000); University and Community Relationships (4000); Program Activities and Member University Involvement (5000); Meetings of the Emeritus College (6000); Program Reports and Communication Activities (7000); Emeritus College Committees (8000), and By-laws (9000).

As previously noted, by-laws are statements related to how the organization will govern itself. The following section (9000) includes the Emeritus College's policies.

9000 BY-LAWS

9100 Emeritus College by-laws are statements of how the Emeritus College will govern itself.

9110 The Emeritus College Council, consisting of nine elected members from the total membership, is considered as the governing body of the Emeritus College and therefore is responsible for developing policy that guides its program activities and enhances the primary goals and objectives of the University.

Monthly meetings of the Council will focus on an agenda that has been determined by the Dean in consultation with the members of the College Council. Parliamentary procedure will be implemented in official Council meetings. Official governance policies will first be considered by the governance committee. A policy must have a first and second reading; whereby the policy is introduced at the first meeting, re-read at the second meeting, and then voted upon at the following meeting for approval or non-approval. Approval requires a majority vote of those present at an official meeting of the council when a quorum is present. A quorum is defined as having six or more voting members present. If a quorum is not present, voting would be carried over to the next meeting of the council.

Emeritus Council Standing Committees' information is set forth in Code 8110.

KEY CHAPTER IDEAS AND RECOMMENDATIONS

- The concept of organizational policy manuals is widespread among the education, business, and industrial organizations of the nation and the world.
- Key sections of effective policy manuals commonly include the primary purposes of the organization, business operations and fiscal management, governance and operational information, hiring procedures, operational procedures, communication measures, personnel requirements, compensation procedures, performance evaluation procedures, attendance and leave provisions, position responsibilities, and personnel relationships.
- Successful organizations tend to name their policy efforts as a primary reason for their success.

- Policy examples from companies such as auto sales and marketing tend to be encouraging for the customers that they serve. That is, positive language is most common.
- The use of numerical codification systems, as opposed to alpha coding systems, appears to be most common in educational and other organizations.
- Note: We did not find a research study concerning the failure of organizations/businesses and whether or not the failing businesses had an ongoing policy plan or not. This finding might be interesting.

REFERENCES

American Friends Service Committee. (2016). *Food Safety & Quality Control Manual.* https://kipdf.com/food-safety-quality-control-manual-january-2016_5ac86d811723dda984e41cfd.html

BankPolicies.com. (2022). *Bank Policy Manual.* https://bankpolicies.com/bank-policy-manual/

Funk, S. (2017). *5 Essential Retail Policies That Will Help Your Business Succeed.* Rain Retail Software website. https://www.rainpos.com/blog/

Gerton Auto Sales, Inc. (2022). *Warranty Information and Terms and Conditions.* https://www.gertonautosales.com/policies-and-procedures

LiveCareer. (2022). *What Is Government Policy?* https: //www.livecareer.com/resources/careers/planning/governance-policies/.

NEOGOV. (2020, December 22). *PowerDMS.* https://www.powerdms.com/cookie-policy

Norton, M. S. (2021). "Policy Manual Codification System for the Arizona State University Emeritus College." Unpublished document.

Waters, S. (2019, June 25). *How to Set Policies and Rules for Your Retail Store.* liveabout.com. https://www.liveabout.com/setting-store-policies-2890473..

Wayne State University Policies (2021). *Policies Manual for Wayne State University.* Board of Regents. Wayne, Nebraska. https://policies.Wayne.edu/.

About the Author

Dr. M. Scott Norton has served as a secondary school teacher of mathematics, coordinator of curriculum for the Lincoln, Nebraska, School District, assistant superintendent for instruction, and superintendent of schools in Salina, Kansas, before joining the University of Nebraska as professor and vice-chair of the Department of Educational Administration and Supervision. Later he served as professor and chair of the Department of Educational Administration and Policy Studies at Arizona State University, where he is professor emeritus. He served militarily in the United States Air Force, where he chaired the Department of Mathematics for the Lackland Educational Preparation School in San Antonio, Texas.

His primary research and instruction areas include educational leadership, human resources administration, teaching methods, governance policy, the assistant school principalship, competency-based administration, the school principalship, research methods, theory, organizational development, organizational change, organizational climate, and educational program improvement. He has published widely in national journals in the areas of teaching/instructional methods, organizational climate, gifted student programs, great teachers, student retention, organizational change, and others. He has published widely on a variety of educational topics for Rowman & Littlefield. He has authored many articles for various professional journals in education, several textbooks on human resources in organizations, and more than 15 books on a variety of educational topics in the professional field of education.

Dr. Norton has received several state and national awards honoring his services and contributions to the field of education and educational administration, including awards from the American Association of School Administrators, the University Council for Educational Administration, The Arizona School Administrators Association, The Nebraska School Administrators Association, The Arizona Educational Research Association, Arizona State College of Education Dean's Award for Distinguished Service to the Field, and the Arizona Information Service, as well as the award for service as President of The College of Education Faculty Association. He recently served a three-year term on the Governance Council for the Emeritus College at Arizona State University.

Dr. Norton's state and national leadership positions have included service as executive director of the Nebraska Association of School Administrators, member of the Board of Directors for the Nebraska Congress of Parents and Teachers, president of the Nebraska Council of Teachers of Mathematics, president of the Arizona School Administrators Higher Education Division, member of the Arizona School Administrators Board of Directors, staff associate for the University Council for Educational Administration, treasurer of the University Council for School Administration, state representative for the Nebraska Association of Secondary School Principals, member of the Board of Editors for the American Association of School Public Relations, recently serving on the Dean's Selection Committee, and member of the governance council for the Arizona State University Emeritus College.

www.ingramcontent.com/pod-product-compliance
Lightning Source LLC
Chambersburg PA
CBHW021717210326
41599CB00013B/1680